A SHEARWATER BOOK

Cities in the Wilderness

Bruce Babbitt

Cities in the Wilderness

A New Vision of Land Use in America

○ **ISLAND**PRESS / **SHEARWATER BOOKS**

Washington · Covelo · London

A Shearwater Book
Published by Island Press

Copyright © 2005 Bruce Babbitt

SHEARWATER BOOKS is a trademark of
The Center for Resource Economics.

Library of Congress Cataloging-in-Publication data.

Babbitt, Bruce E.
  Cities in the wilderness : a new vision of land use in America / Bruce Babbitt.
    p. cm.
  Includes bibliographical references and index.
  ISBN 1-55963-093-0 (cloth : alk. paper)
    1. Land use — United States — Planning. 2. Land use — Government policy —
  United States. 3. Wilderness areas — United States — Management. 4. Nature
  conservation — United States. 5. Land use — Environmental aspects — United
  States.   I. Title: New vision of land use in America.   II. Title: Land use in
  America.   III. Title.
    HD205.B32   2005
    333.73'17'0973 — dc22

                                        2005017198

British Cataloguing-in-Publication data available.

Printed on recycled, acid-free paper ✇

Design by David Bullen Design

Manufactured in the United States of America

10 9 8 7 6 5 4 3 2 1

For Hattie, David Hayes,
John Leshy, and Anne Shields,
my partners through the Interior years

Contents

And the Lord spoke to Moses in the plains of Moab by the Jordan across from Jericho, saying: "Command the children of Israel that they give the Levites cities to dwell in. . . . The common-land of the cities which you will give the Levites shall extend from the wall of the city outward a thousand cubits all around."

NUMBERS 35:1–4

Cities in the Wilderness

Prologue

IT WAS A COLD November day in 1997 when I traveled to Pennsylvania to commemorate the anniversary of Lincoln's Gettysburg Address. The ridges along the battlefield stood out sharp and clear in the morning light as a brisk wind scattered fallen leaves across the frozen fields. After the ceremony we toured the battlefield accompanied by the British military historian John Keegan. We began by tracing the Confederate battle line southward, stopping frequently to look across the fields at the imposing heights of Cemetery Ridge, trying to imagine the emotions as Pickett and his men awaited orders to storm across the open fields and up the heights toward the entrenched Union troops.

We reached the south end of the Confederate line, where Keegan took us back to events of July 2, 1863, the day before Pickett's charge. He pointed out Little Round Top, the rocky hill that had anchored the Union left. We crossed the field, climbed over boulders, and pushed through the oak trees up the slope where the 20th Maine had been rushed down the Union line to hold the hill against a flanking Confederate attack. Outnumbered, a third of his men out of action, Colonel Joshua Chamberlain organized the defense. When ammunition ran out the colonel rallied his men and ordered them to fix bayonets and charge straight into the gunfire of the oncoming Alabamans. Startled by the ferocity of the attack, the exhausted Confederates surrendered and the Union line held.

Absorbed in Keegan's description of the carnage and the unimaginable heroism, I glanced up through the trees, and then I saw it—a giant structure resembling an air traffic control tower looming over the battlefield. I tried to concentrate on the story of Chamberlain and the 20th Maine, but the spell was broken and the past dissolved into the present. An observation tower? How did it get there? Why had the Park Service ever countenanced such a monstrous desecration of this battlefield?

We paused on a ledge, and the park superintendent explained. Back in 1963 a developer had purchased land and submitted a proposal to build a tower that would allow visitors to overlook the entire battlefield for a fee. Park advocates had objected, arguing that this national battlefield, above all others, should be preserved pristine, free from commercial intrusion. But in the end the developer's private-property rights prevailed. The losers would be the millions of visitors coming each year to Gettysburg seeking an authentic experience and remembrance of the three bloody days that had saved the Union.

Several years after that initial visit I returned to Gettysburg in July to observe the anniversary of the battle. This day was hot and humid, rain clouds moving on the horizon, just as it had been back in 1863. We reviewed the reenactor troops lined up with their cannon; spread out with the giant tower in the background they seemed diminished to the scale of toy soldiers on a game board. We heard an order to fire, the cannon boomed, and clouds of smoke spread across the field. And then a series of answering explosions came from the edge of the battlefield. The tower buckled, swayed to the right, hung in midair for a moment, and then, to the cheers of soldiers and onlookers, crumpled into the clouds of smoke.

It had taken yet another battle, this one in the Congress, to bring the tower down. For years a coalition of park supporters, Civil War enthusiasts, and the National Trust for Historic Preservation had lobbied Congress to approve and fund removal of the tower. Gettysburg, we argued, is more than just a collection of monuments, markers, and plaques; it is an historic landscape that to be understood must be seen whole, as the participants saw it on those fateful days in 1863 and as the generals, converging upon the site, saw the topography, framed their strategies, and deployed their troops. It is hard to visualize General Lee riding in from the west on July 1, passing in sight of a twenty-five-story steel tower.

The developers replied that they had complied with the law by obtaining all the necessary permits. But the question remained— should the national interest of all Americans in preserving this sacred site be left exclusively to the discretion of a local planning commission? And should that decision, once made, be allowed to stand forever, accorded the same permanence as the battlefield itself?

Eventually Congress agreed with our view of the national interest, and ultimately the Park Service settled the matter by paying the owner several million dollars for a structure that should never have been permitted in the first place. Yet even as that tower came crashing down, we were losing out in the broader struggle to preserve the nation's history. Half an hour from Gettysburg, Antietam, the scene of the greatest one-day casualty toll in American history, was under siege on three sides by subdivisions. Across the Potomac at the Manassas battlefield, road builders and mall developers were closing in from two sides. All up and down the Shenandoah Valley, where the great Civil War cavalry battles had raged, strip malls, roads, gas stations, and subdivisions were spreading across the land.

It is not just Civil War battlefields that are threatened by sprawl, of course. Across the country entire landscapes, seacoasts, river valleys, and forests are disappearing, covered over by highways, housing developments, and shopping malls. The ongoing destruction of the American landscape is so well-known as to beggar extensive description. The facts are plain to anyone who drives from San Diego to Los Angeles, or travels the east coast of Florida, or down from Boston through New York to Washington, or along the highways that line the banks of our rivers, or who has entered a national park through the cultural junkyards known as "gateway communities." You can see the evidence almost anywhere in America by simply traveling outward from a city center into the surrounding rural landscapes. And with each passing year these trends are accelerating, driven by the relentless pressures of increasing population and resource consumption.

Only rarely, though, do these threatened and defiled landscapes become a national issue of sufficient interest to prompt Congress to act, and only then if the threat is to a well-known, popular park like Gettysburg or Yellowstone. And even on those infrequent occasions when Congress does intervene, it typically leaves the task half finished. In 1994 a Canadian gold-mining company announced plans to mine a mountain peak on the border of Yellowstone National Park. The ensuing public outcry prompted Congress to appropriate sixty-three million dollars to buy out and revoke the mining claim. The president came to celebrate, but even as he spoke, just a few miles away thousands of acres of habitat essential for bison and other park wildlife were being carved up by subdividers selling vacation sites along the park boundary.

The factors behind our disappearing landscapes and dwindling rivers are no mystery. They were brought to public attention back in the 1960s by the writer William Whyte and by others who described the relentless building of highways, including the interstate highway system, as the spearhead of landscape destruction, with land speculators and developers following as the concrete hardens and the asphalt cools. They explained how government policies subsidize sprawl and noted that local officials, with rare exception, seem unwilling or unable to stand up to the onrushing forces of development.

It is not my intention simply to add another hand-wringing lamentation to the chorus of studies that detail our failures at rational land use planning. Why demonize land developers when the real problem is the pervasive failure of state and local governments to control sprawl through meaningful land use regulations? The problem lies within us and our political institutions. Local governments generally have neither the political will nor the expertise nor the financial resources to stand up to well-financed developers demanding "just one more exception," while lubricating their requests with political contributions. And the occasional local government that does attempt effective planning often loses out, unable to influence what happens just outside the city limits or across the county line, where the jurisdiction with the least environmental regulations often prevails in the competition for jobs and tax revenue.

The purpose of this book, instead, is to show how we can prevent the loss of natural and cultural landscapes and watersheds through stronger federal leadership in land use planning. It may come as something of a surprise to learn there is such a thing as "federal land use planning." The notion that land use is a local matter has come to dominate the political rhetoric of our age, obscuring the historical reality that the national government has been involved in land use planning since the early days of the republic. In fact, there is, by whatever name, a considerable body of law that can and, in my view, should be used toward enhanced federal leadership in land use planning and preservation.

The case for federal leadership in land use planning must begin with a consideration of exactly what the national interest consists of. No one, for example, suggests that Congress should be concerned with street patterns in a suburban development or the location of schools or public facilities in your community. But most of us would agree that the national government should be concerned with protecting disappearing species, the integrity of rivers that cross state lines, our coastlines, our forests, and regions of special significance for their scenic, ecological, or historic values. Yet with few exceptions we have not engaged in a national discussion of how to define that interest, where to draw the lines, and how to involve the states in the process.

In this book I make the case for federal leadership in making land use regulation work more effectively in this country. I have selected examples to illustrate specific success stories, to suggest how these successes can be applied more generally to all regions of the country, and in some cases, to argue the need for additional federal legislation. These stories draw upon my experience as governor of Arizona and then as secretary of the interior and they come from many regions of the country, as diverse as south Florida, Chesapeake Bay, the Missouri River Basin, Iowa, the Pacific Northwest, California, and, of course, Arizona. They have been selected and dissected with the aim of persuading the reader that not only do we have a viable tradition of federal engagement in land use, but that the strands of past success should now be drawn together into a coherent national land use policy.

The Florida Everglades represents our most notorious example of a great national park nearly destroyed by highways, water diversions, encroaching development, and agricultural conversion. The area has now become the subject of the largest restoration project ever authorized by Congress, and at the heart of this effort is a comprehensive land use planning initiative for the entire Everglades watershed extending down the Florida peninsula from Lake Okeechobee to the waters of Florida Bay.

In chapter 1, I consider the Everglades experience at some length, attempting to answer, or at least shed some light on, several important questions: Why has the state of Florida been so receptive to federal leadership in regional land use planning? What motivated Congress, generally hostile to environmental initiatives during the 1990s, to make such a large, unprecedented commitment to regional planning and environmental restoration? Could the Florida experience be the harbinger of a new national commitment to land use planning and ecosystem restoration? Or was it a one time occurrence precipitated by a random accumulation of rare events, unlikely to recur anytime soon?

Chapter 2 examines the Endangered Species Act, which, although not usually characterized as a land use planning statute, has become one of the most effective federal laws affecting land use. It has been most successful in California, in large measure because that state government, through both Republican and Democratic administrations, has worked out a partnership with the federal government for regional open space planning.

Here I focus on the Southern California success story that emerged from a crucible of conflict occasioned by the listing of an endangered bird, the California gnatcatcher. That in turn triggered a land development moratorium and led eventually to a pattern of cooperation on land use that has since been extended to other regions of California. From California, I move on to Las Vegas, Tucson, and several other urban areas where the federal government has played a substantial role in land use, and I suggest how the Endangered Species Act could be extended to encourage protection of critical ecosystems and open space throughout the country.

Chapter 3 takes us to the Midwest, a part of the country whose natural history has been largely ignored and forgotten, even by the people who reside there. The farmlands of this region, planted fencerow to fencerow, have obliterated the tallgrass prairie, which lives on only in memory and in small patches in old cemeteries. The vast fields of corn and soybeans have so completely preempted and displaced the old prairie that the natural world seems to have vanished beyond any realistic hope of retrieval.

Ironically, the historical emergence of this region of all-consuming industrial agriculture is due in large measure to federal land use policies. Farm country is one place where no one disputes either the reality or the necessity of federal leadership in land use, even though it goes by the name of "farm policy." Federal farm policy has influenced use of the land since the beginning of the Republic, nearly always directed toward expanding production through the draining, clearing, and planting of more land.

Now, however, farm policy is nearing the threshold of a revolutionary change, made necessary by the globalization of the agricultural economy and emergence of the World Trade Organization as the arbiter of agricultural policies that subsidize prices and encourage overproduction. In coming years, the United States will be required to begin dismantling production subsidies, which reach as high as fifteen billion dollars or more per year. As these production subsidies are withdrawn, there will be an unprecedented opportunity to redirect this money to permanent retirement of marginal farmlands and to restore a network of forested riparian corridors across the land, and even to bring back extensive tracts of the old tallgrass prairie, all in a manner designed to continue providing income and support to farmers.

In farming regions and in urban areas, land use is reflected in the waters. Improper management of the land has seriously degraded our rivers and lakes and estuaries. Chapter 4 looks at Chesapeake Bay, a large estuary that collects the waters running off the land from six states. The streams and rivers that drain this watershed are contaminated from farmland fertilizers, pesticides, animal waste, the destruction of forests, and residues from urban streets. In consequence the bay is nearing ecological collapse. The once abundant oyster reefs are crumbling, and the once extensive beds of sea grass that shelter and nourish spawning blue crabs are dying, smothered by sediments that accumulate as soils erode, having been exposed by deforestation and excessive tillage. Oyster and crab catches have declined to less than 1 percent of historic levels. Similar declines in fisheries are occurring in every region of the country.

The Clean Water Act, which mandates the restoration of our waters to a "fishable and swimmable" standard, has proven inadequate to the task, in large measure because after thirty years of effort federal administrators and the courts have been unable to bring the states forward as effective partners in the regulation of land use to restore the nation's waters. From an examination of these shortcomings and the ways water policies have affected the growth and development of cities, I argue in chapter 4 that the Clean Water Act should be revised to promote stronger federal-state partnerships in managing the use of water resources and in regulating the effects of land use on our rivers and lakes.

In the concluding chapter I return to my western roots to discuss the past and future of our public lands. These lands, the flamboyant red-rock landscapes of Arizona and Utah, the distinctive life forms of the Sonoran and Mojave deserts, the towering forests of the Rockies and the Pacific Northwest, the lands of Alaska, are a unique and enduring part of our heritage. They are also a perpetual battleground, where the gun smoke of endless political fights obscures both the meaning of the past and the prospects for the future. For a hundred years, ranchers, miners, and loggers have fought with conservationists, one side seeking to throw the lands open to oil drilling, logging, livestock grazing, and strip mining while the other would have extractive uses excluded, with all the lands protected as the equivalent of national parks.

After eight years of intense participation in these battles as secretary of the interior and subsequent years of observing from the sidelines, I believe the time has come for an armistice followed by a peace conference to which not just westerners, but all Americans, are invited. The outcome should be a new constitution for public lands, in the form of federal legislation that subordinates (but does not eliminate) mining, grazing, and logging to an overriding public mandate for long-term biological diversity, abundant wildlife and fisheries, and the ecological integrity of our streams and watersheds.

RECENTLY I WENT BACK again to Gettysburg, much in the way I return again and again to the Grand Canyon and Yosemite, never failing to appreciate even more of their beauty and meaning. Again walking the battlefield, I was pleased to find no trace of the tower; the wreckage had all been carted away, the foundations removed, and the land carefully restored by the Park Service.

On this visit, however, I was not searching out specific sites; now that the distraction of the tower was gone, I wanted to understand the entire landscape of battle from the perspective of the participants. How, I wondered, had the opposing forces come to select and occupy the positions from which the great battles would emerge? How had the Union managed to dominate the battlefield by occupying the heights of Cemetery Ridge, even before Generals Lee and Meade had arrived to take command of their respective armies?

What I discovered was another of those leadership lessons of the Civil War—this one a lesson in good land use planning. On the afternoon of June 30, 1863, during the initial skirmishes, a Union colonel had spotted Culp's Hill, grasped its significance, and occupied it. Then General Winfield Scott Hancock, arriving to take interim command, made what would be the fateful land use decisions, informed by what a contemporary characterized as "a wonderfully quick and correct eye for ground." Swiftly comprehending the larger landscape and its interrelated parts, Hancock directed a rapid, unopposed deployment all the way along Cemetery Ridge to

Little Round Top on the south end. By the time Lee and Meade arrived to take charge of their forces, the framework for the battles had been set.

Landowners, developers, farmers, planners, historic preservationists, conservationists—wherever we reside, in cities, in suburbs, or in rural areas, we must all begin to comprehend our surroundings as landscapes and watersheds. We must explore what they mean in our lives and determine how to live in and use them while conserving their essential functions, passing them intact and unimpaired to future generations.

I

Everglades Forever

IN SOUTH FLORIDA, hurricanes are the prime movers of land use planning. Periodically a big storm comes in off the Atlantic, smashing forests, wrecking roads and buildings, and flooding the land. Then, as the wreckage is piled up and carted away, there is a moment of opportunity to build something different, incorporating lessons learned from the storm, avoiding mistakes of the past, and even implementing new ideas of how to live in harmony with the constraints imposed by the land and the climate. Hurricanes, for all the human tragedy, bring opportunities for urban renewal.

It was in the summer of 1992 that I began to learn about hurricanes and renewal. In August of that year Hurricane Andrew blew ashore just south of Miami, leading with a seventeen-foot storm surge, followed by winds exceeding one hundred and seventy miles per hour. By most accounts it was the most powerful hurricane of the century, and as it moved inland it left a wide trail of destruction, leaving nearly two hundred thousand residents temporarily homeless.

On its way inland, Andrew demolished Homestead Air Force Base, located about twenty miles south of Miami near the tip of the Florida peninsula. Suddenly more than five thousand workers from the surrounding Cuban, Haitian, and Latino communities were left jobless. The Air Force added to their despair several months later by announcing that Homestead would not be rebuilt. The abandoned site, several thousand acres, would instead be made available for commercial redevelopment. But that was by no means the end of proposals for the area. Hurricane Andrew had opened up an opportunity for planners to take a fresh look at the future of the region. As pressures mounted to generate jobs by rebuilding, a group of Cuban Americans with close ties to the county commissioners proposed to take over Homestead and develop a jetport, dedicated to air cargo, that would draw industry and distribution facilities from throughout the Americas.

Florida environmentalists immediately objected. The Homestead site was adjacent to Biscayne National Park and a mere eleven miles from the entrance to Everglades National Park. A commercial airport would attract more freeways and sprawl, inevitably degrading both parks. South Miami-Dade, opponents argued, should become a transition zone of low-density residential development feathering out to open space as it approached the aquamarine waters of Biscayne Bay and the saw grass swamps of the Everglades. And since Homestead was a federal facility, environmental advocates expected the federal government to take the lead in promoting their vision of appropriate development.

Then suddenly, mysteriously, the debate was terminated. Within weeks the Miami-Dade County Commission voted unanimously to recommend that the Homestead site be transferred to their friends, the industrial jetport advocates. No hearings were held and no opportunity was given for public comment. No alternative plans were offered or considered. Word on the street was that the deal had the support of the president of the United States.

Angry opponents of the jetport had nowhere to go, at least for the time being. Back in Washington, other issues, such as the budget, health care, and gays in the military were occupying the press and Congress. But Florida's environmentalists were not about to go quietly. And they had long memories, certainly extending back to 1976 when, after a prolonged public battle, they had successfully blocked a jetport west of Miami in what subsequently became the Big Cypress National Preserve section of the Everglades. As we shall see, opponents of the Homestead jetport would return to the issue in the 2000 presidential election campaign.

While these controversies were developing, another less spectacular disaster was slowly spreading across the Everglades itself, that vast wetland region about the size of Puerto Rico or Jamaica that occupies the southern end of the Florida peninsula. The cause was not a hurricane, but a relentless wave of subdivisions, industrial development, and agriculture moving inland from the coastlines, encircling and constricting the wetlands, draining away the waters, drying the land and killing off the water-dependent wildlife. The signs of starvation were everywhere, especially in the decline of the wading-bird populations that once graced the landscape. Visiting the region after taking office as secretary of the interior, I canoed through the mangrove swamps for hours without spotting more than one or two white egrets soaring among the towering banks of cumulus clouds. Then suddenly I would come upon a roosting tree, weighed down with birds so thick that the branches seemed covered with snowfall, a rare sighting of what was once commonplace. But most of the time the skies were empty, and I would wait many hours to spot an endangered Everglades kite cruising over the land in search of apple snails in the diminished stands of saw grass.

Everglades National Park is a relatively large park, about a million acres, but it is nonetheless a small part, less than 25 percent, of the original Everglades ecosystem. Exactly why a national park of this size and extent should be in such trouble was not immediately apparent. Since I was not eager to see the park's ecosystem collapse and species go extinct on my watch, I flew to south Florida intent on discovering what the Park Service was doing wrong, and to correct the problem. I soon learned, however, that the Park Service was not to blame. The Everglades could not be fixed by appointing a new superintendent or adding more rangers or posting more signs asking visitors not to feed the wildlife. The source of the problem was not even in the park; it originated a hundred miles upstream, far outside park boundaries.

THE EVERGLADES is a vast wetland, so shallow and so flat that it resembles a tallgrass prairie. But it is in fact a river, a very wide stream of very slow-moving water that was once connected to Lake Okeechobee, a huge inland lake a hundred miles to the north that in turn is fed by the Kissimmee River, which originates in a string of shallow central Florida lakes. The sheet flows of water that sustained the lands within the park originally ebbed and flowed in a seasonal cycle fed by summer rains and by the waters stored in Lake Okeechobee and on the land itself. The wildlife of the Everglades — the alligators, crocodiles, panthers, bears, the wading birds, and the plant life — all evolved and adapted to the intricate seasonal cycles of flowing water.

In the nineteenth century, Florida settlers moved inland from the coast and began draining the lands around Lake Okeechobee to farm. Soon the hydrologic connection between the lake and the Everglades began to dry up. More wetlands were lost to limestone mining and to subdivision development. In 1928 completion of the Tamiami Trail, an elevated roadway from Miami to Florida's west coast, created the equivalent of a fifty-mile dike across the heart of the remaining Everglades, breaking up and disrupting the sheet flows across the land. By 1990 more than half of the original flows into the Everglades had been diverted and drained away.

The initial boundaries of Everglades National Park were set in 1947, at a time when much less was known about the complex hydrology of wetland ecosystems and the rivers that feed into them. Park planners concentrated their gaze and their pencils on the land, not the water, and they assumed that a million acres — about the size of a big western national park like Grand Canyon or Yosemite — would be sufficient to preserve the character of the region and its wildlife.

It was becoming increasingly clear by the 1990s that those assumptions were wrong. The notion that the Everglades could function as an isolated remnant of the original ecosystem was mistaken. The national park, located at the terminus of the watershed, where the waters discharge into Florida Bay, is dependent upon upstream waters flowing south from the Lake Okeechobee region. As development spread into south-central Florida, more lands were drained, cutting off the park increasingly from its upstream sources of water. To save the park we would have to restore some semblance of the original flows by reconnecting waterways northward toward Lake Okeechobee.

Recognizing the need to reconnect the severed sheet flows meant acknowledging that development had already taken too large a share of the land and waters of the natural ecosystem. To restore adequate flows meant taking water back from existing agricultural uses, filling in drainage canals, and allowing some farms to revert to swampland. And it would be necessary to halt further encroachment by purchasing or condemning thousands of undeveloped subdivision lots within the natural floodways that bring water into the park.

These restoration ideas, premised on the notion that some development had gone too far and should now be reversed, were largely without precedent in conservation history. For a hundred years conservation had been about preservation—setting aside and protecting land before it was lost to development. Now we were looking at taking land back from development; and that sounded like a zero-sum game, taking from one side to give to the other. As a society, we have always assumed that land, once occupied, was ours, forever lost to the natural world, no matter how great the environmental damage that occupancy might cause. Even as development sprawled across the land, obliterating natural systems, hardly anything ever went the other way, back to nature, except a few crumbling ghost towns near abandoned gold mines in the western deserts.

To restore the Everglades we would have to challenge the assumption that permanent conquest and occupancy always resulted in a good outcome, no matter the land's location or its use. We would have to organize a retreat from occupied territory, yielding the conquered land back to its original inhabitants. It was a new concept, sure to invoke fierce opposition.

Yet as open spaces have disappeared, as development has accelerated and the patterns of sprawl have spread across the nation, it has become clear that in many areas development has already undermined the integrity of surrounding natural systems—not just in the Everglades, or in great parks like Grand Canyon and Yellowstone, but also along the California coast, in the foothills of the Sierra Nevada, in the Front Range of the Rockies, in the Chesapeake Bay region, and along most of the country's rivers. In the fast-growing coastal regions of Maryland and Virginia, the destruction of forest cover and polluted runoff from cities and farms has nearly destroyed the Chesapeake's once abundant oyster and crab fisheries. On the other side of the country, in San Diego County, more than a hundred species of plants, mammals, and birds have been identified as threatened or endangered due to habitat destruction from expanding subdivisions. In the Pacific Northwest, in New

England, many of the legendary native salmon stocks are declining toward extinction because of forest clearing, dam building, sprawling developments, and overextension of agriculture. Throughout the Midwest the tallgrass prairie ecosystems are virtually a thing of the past. It is time to weigh the benefits of marginal developments against the damage they might cause to surrounding ecosystems and to think seriously about changing the proportions between human space and wild space.

Faced with the shriveling Everglades ecosystem, embarking upon a restoration program would require the Department of the Interior to ask Congress for authorizing legislation and large appropriations to finance the work. This would mean asking Congress to help us open a new chapter in conservation history at the very time that political tides were running in the opposite direction: in the early and mid-1990s Congress was considering proposals to close national parks, to weaken the Clean Water Act, and to eviscerate the Endangered Species Act. We could not count on support from the White House. The president was caught up in protracted disputes over the budget and health care, and even in the best of times, he had never been greatly interested in environmental issues.

Outside Washington, property-rights activists were in the ascendancy, manifested by crowds of demonstrators who turned out almost everywhere I went, from New Hampshire to California. Florida, however, seemed an exception. The Florida press was alive with stories of the Everglades imperiled, detailing the deterioration of the ecosystem, the virtual disappearance of the Florida panther, the decline in wading-bird populations, and the extent of polluted water flowing from the sugar fields. Most remarkably, the Florida press was calling for federal leadership in resolving the Everglades' plight. This at the same time that, in most parts of the country, I was confronting a rising tide of antigovernment opinion, fueled by Newt Gingrich and other conservatives who would soon win control of Congress. Why, I wondered, was Florida so different?

In March 1993 I went to Fort Myers to speak to the Everglades Coalition, an umbrella group of environmental organizations calling for Everglades restoration. I endorsed their wish list, which included land acquisition, cracking down on the sugar companies, and undertaking a comprehensive study of the region's plumbing system, that vast network of dikes, pumps, and canals that extended across south Florida diverting and draining away water before it could reach the Everglades.

I was still skeptical, however, that anything could come of this group's ambitious proposals, which I estimated would cost billions of dollars, when Congress was cutting budgets right and left. Even in the most expansive times, during a New Deal or the Great Society, a program of this magnitude would have been a tall order. But there was one thing about the audience that caught my attention and made me think twice about the chances for success. Sprinkled among the predictable attendees—young activists and elderly retirees—were some influential investment bankers and real-estate developers.

Among these was Nathaniel Reed, a lean, ruddy, aristocratic sportsman, proprietor of an upscale enclave at Hobe Sound on the Atlantic coast. Reed had been an assistant secretary of the interior in the Nixon administration, which initially gave me pause about his intentions. I soon discovered, however, that Reed was a Republican in the spirit of Theodore Roosevelt, passionately committed to environmental causes, the foremost being the Everglades. He would become one of my most trusted outside advisors.

In evenings over dinner on the terrace of his home on Hobe Sound, Reed expounded on the bond between Florida residents and the Everglades. Most of the people living in south Florida, he explained, were newcomers who migrated south to live in the tropics by choice. "And they are not about to sit by and watch it disappear," he claimed. "In Florida the Everglades transcends politics. Everyone supports the Everglades — except big sugar."

You could say much the same about the Grand Canyon in my home state, I replied. In Arizona everybody loves the canyon. It's an icon; you see it plastered on everything from T-shirts to license plates to backdrops in television commercials. But that did not prevent the state's governor from vilifying the Park Service and opposing efforts to protect the park. Reed shrugged, "All I can tell you is Florida is different."

I eventually concluded that some of that Florida difference lay buried in the state's long history of contending with hurricane disasters and the nature of the land. My instructor here was Marjory Stoneman Douglas, through her book *The Everglades: River of Grass*. In it she chronicles the struggle by early settlers to come to grips with the overwhelming reality of the swamps and the region's violent tropical storms, efforts that eventually led residents into a mutually beneficial land management partnership with the federal government and the Army Corps of Engineers.

AT THE TIME of European arrival in the region, the Everglades covered most of what is now south Florida in shallow expanses of water. Early settlers moving inland from the Atlantic coast wrote of them as pestilent, mosquito-infested swamps just waiting to be drained and plowed into productive farmland. These early settlers eventually learned, however, that no amount of individual effort would be sufficient to subdue the land. It was impossible to drain a forty-acre tract in order to farm in the middle of a swamp. And even local community efforts, undertaken in the spirit of a New England barn raising, could not create farmland in the middle of an ocean of water that extended to the horizon in every direction. Transforming swamps into farms would require government help.

The first step was taken in Washington. In 1850 Congress

enacted the Swamplands Act, which offered to divest federal title to swamplands to the states, provided the states in question would agree to drain and transform them into farmland. Florida accepted the offer and ignored the condition. Taking title to vast tracts of the Everglades, the state then handed the lands over to politically connected speculators who promised to assume the state's obligation to drain the lands.

Speculators, in turn also ignoring the drainage obligation, created paper subdivisions and mounted campaign to sell lots to out-of-state buyers ignorant of the true condition of the land. By the beginning of the twentieth century these land-promotion schemes were collapsing in a boom and bust economic cycle (although only temporarily, it would turn out), and voters began clamoring for the state to take direct charge of a drainage program. An energetic Miami businessman named Napoleon Bonaparte Broward stepped forward to run for governor on a drain-the-swamps platform. He had a knack for analogies: if the Dutch could push back the North Sea to reclaim land that lay *below* sea level, he argued, it should be easy for the people of Florida to drain water from the Everglades, where the swamps were perched *above* sea level, by simply pulling the plug.

The voters agreed. After taking office in 1906, Broward persuaded the Florida legislature to establish a Board of Drainage Commissioners armed with the power of eminent domain and authority to levy a drainage tax of up to five cents an acre for dredging canals to sluice the waters out to sea. Within months, work gangs were blasting through the rock ledges along the Atlantic, and dredges were working their way inland digging giant drainage canals. Still, even with Broward's energetic leadership, the conquest of the swamps proved slow going. The soft peat soils often turned to syrup, slumping into the canals and clogging streams. Primitive dredges frequently broke down, and workers fell sick in the relentless tropical sun.

Despite the difficulties, the program gradually produced results. The waters began draining out to sea, seeming to validate Broward's boast that Florida could easily conquer the swamps and reclaim the land. Then several disasters struck. In 1926 a powerful hurricane tracked in off the Atlantic, ripping a swath across the peninsula, destroying thousands of homes and inundating most of the laboriously reclaimed farmlands. The waters receded, the lands dried, and homes were eventually rebuilt. Two years later another monster storm swept inland, this time north of Fort Lauderdale, taking dead aim at Lake Okeechobee. When winds of the counter-clockwise swirl hit the lake, giant waves of water poured southward over the rim and across the Everglades, once again inundating the land. This time more than two thousand people were swept away and drowned beneath the waves.

In the aftermath of the Okeechobee disaster, Florida made an anguished plea for federal help. Congress responded by instructing the Army Corps of Engineers to isolate Lake Okeechobee from the rest of the Everglades by building a huge earthen dike along the lake's southern shore, sufficient to contain a storm surge from even the largest hurricane. The Hoover Dike, as it came to be known, was supplemented by lateral canals to drain waters east to the Atlantic and west to the Gulf of Mexico. It was a portentous beginning to an enduring federal-state partnership in the management of lands threatened by flooding.

As life in the region returned to normal and development continued to advance inland, disaster struck again. In 1947 two back-to-back hurricanes once again flooded the region, leaving more than 90 percent of south Florida under water, prompting the president to declare an emergency and the governor to call out the National Guard to patrol affected coastal cities. Florida once again turned to Washington, seeking an expanded federal role in the unending struggle to harden the land against incoming hurricanes.

So the planners began again. By this time, however, the notion of simply escalating an all-out campaign to conquer the land by draining swamps and expanding agriculture was yielding to a more complex vision. Florida in the postwar years was becoming an urban state, and fast-growing cities like Miami and Fort Lauderdale on the Atlantic coast became interested, not in draining the swamps, but in keeping water in place to recharge the freshwater aquifers from which these municipalities pumped increasing quantities of water.

Environmentalists and sportsmen also campaigned for preserving rather than draining off the swamps, increasingly known by the less pejorative term "wetlands." The Audubon Society joined with other groups and individuals to advocate the creation of a new Everglades national park to protect the wading birds, the Florida panther, and wildlife endemic to the wetland ecosystem.

In 1948 Congress authorized the Army Corps of Engineers to prepare an expanded flood-control and water-management plan for the region. Working with the state, the Corps developed a new, hybrid landscape vision. The old drain-the-swamps model was discarded in favor of a partition plan designed to satisfy each of the major stakeholders. The Everglades ecosystem would be divided into three distinct parts: a third to be drained for the sugar plantations, a third to store water for the cities, and a third for nature.

The laws of gravity and hydrology dictated the design and location of the three sections. Although the Everglades is a sea of grass, it is also a river, albeit an unusual river, miles wide and inches deep flowing slowly across land that slopes a mere two inches per mile. The headwaters around Lake Okeechobee were the easiest to deal with, evidenced by some previously drained and planted land in that area. The new plan expanded on that nucleus, enlarging the system of canals leading southward and eastward to the Atlantic and constructing pumping plants to irrigate the fields directly from

Lake Okeechobee in time of drought. In the process the plan expanded agricultural land to more than a million acres.

Immediately south of the agricultural area, the planners reserved a million acres for water storage to recharge underground aquifers for the benefit of the growing Atlantic-coast cities. These water conservation areas would also capture and retain irrigation water draining off the sugar plantations. To store water on the surface to a depth of five to six feet, the Corps enclosed large tracts of the wetlands with earthen dikes that ran for miles across the landscape. From the air they resembled the huge intaglio patterns left by vanished civilizations in the Peruvian deserts.

Conservationists got the leftovers, mostly located in the southern portion of the watershed, in the "delta" where the waters converge into Florida Bay. This was the most remote and wild section of the Everglades remaining, the least affected by human development. Congress had authorized a national park back in 1934, but the park did not come into being until 1947 when President Truman came to south Florida to dedicate it. In his speech the president accurately and presciently described the hydrological reality that would eventually threaten the very existence of this new Everglades National Park: "Here is land tranquil in its quiet beauty, serving not as the source of water, but as the last receiver of it."

This trifecta partition required hydraulic engineering on an unprecedented scale to keep the water moving steadily downstream through the system, draining the land at the top for agriculture, collecting and storing water in the middle for the cities, and then releasing sufficient flows downstream to meet the varying seasonal needs of the park. And once completed, the system would require continuing intensive management. Accordingly, the Corps and the state of Florida agreed to a permanent Everglades partnership. The Corps would build and operate the major canals and pump stations. The Florida legislature would form the South Florida Water

Management Agency, granting it administrative and taxing powers over the entire watershed, including authority to distribute the water pursuant to state law. The two partners, federal and state, would share the costs fifty-fifty.

As I BECAME AWARE of this history I began to think that I had been too skeptical about contemporary prospects for Everglades restoration. Perhaps such a major effort would have a chance. Among states, Florida was different, and its history of violent storms and flooding clearly had much to do with that. Each episode of storm and destruction had given rise to new restoration and reconstruction initiatives. Florida residents had experienced the fragility and impermanence of the developed landscape and were more aware than most people of the constraints imposed by the natural world. In consequence, they were more open to considering new visions of their relation to the land.

Floridians, by virtue of this history, had also come to accept, and indeed to demand, federal leadership in the planning and management of their land and water. Twice in the twentieth century the state and the Army Corps of Engineers had collaborated to rearrange the landscape on a grand scale. Now, we in the federal government were proposing to do it once again. In light of this history, such an undertaking did not seem unfamiliar or objectionable. All that was really new this time was our introduction of a new priority—the primacy of restoring the natural systems of the Everglades. But even this change of direction could be understood in the context of a continual evolution of Florida's relation with the land, from conquest, to partition, and now toward a broader emphasis on protecting the natural landscape.

It remained only to insinuate this change of direction into the bureaucratic mentality of our federal partner, the Army Corps of Engineers. This was perhaps the most daunting challenge, for if Florida history provided cause for optimism, the long history of the

Corps suggested a rocky transition. For two centuries the Corps had been the institutional embodiment of the American idea that progress always followed the axe and the plow. The Corps had employed industrial technology and the resources of the national government to conquer the most unruly forces of nature, the rivers that flooded so unpredictably across the land. And, in a nation in thrall to large-scale public works, the Corps would proceed with little concern for what was being lost in the process.

As we began to formulate a plan for Everglades restoration, our bureaucratic task in Washington loomed large. To restore the Everglades we would have to reform the Corps. We would have to persuade the Corps, and its many friends in Congress, that Americans were ready for a better balance between development and the protection of natural systems and that achieving that balance could include undoing damage caused by pushing development so indiscriminately in the past.

One problem was that as secretary of the interior I did not have jurisdiction over the Corps, an agency buried deep within the Department of Defense, where it was so insignificant in size relative to other branches of the military that I wondered whether the secretary of defense even knew of its existence. There was no alternative but to try to win over those directly in charge of the agency. In the summer of 1993, I invited the commanding general to meet in my office. We brought out the good china, and I retold the story of how the secretary of the interior came to occupy an office several times larger than the Oval Office. At the beginning of the New Deal one of my predecessors, Harold Ickes, confidant of Franklin D. Roosevelt and director of the Works Progress Administration, decided to build a new Interior building. In the process he sent his architect around Washington to look at every office occupied by a cabinet secretary, giving instructions to add several feet to the largest dimensions encountered.

Pleasantries exchanged, we turned to a discussion of what an

Everglades initiative might actually entail. It could be, I suggested, a risky venture for both of us. Environmentalists considered the Corps an agency beyond redemption, guilty of destroying more than 90 percent of the wetlands in the contiguous forty-eight states through its relentless advocacy of dredging, drainage, and dam-building projects. Their idea of interagency collaboration was to abolish the Corps and distribute its functions to the Environmental Protection Agency, the Department of the Interior, and to other government agencies more sensitive to the environment.

I also acknowledged the risks to the Corps of a partnership with a secretary, already considered too aggressive by some in Congress, in something as new and untested as the restoration of an entire ecosystem. And then I made the sales pitch. This was an unexcelled opportunity for the Corps to make a difference in the future direction of the country. It would be a chance for the Corps to broaden its public appeal and to develop new constituencies in Congress and in the states. And, finally, I suggested that Everglades restoration was a high priority for our new administration, which intended to be around this town for many more years.

The general listened carefully and seemed interested, but he was not rushing into anything as momentous as this. He explained that any new initiative would have to be developed by following traditional procedures. Congress would first have to authorize a feasibility study that normally would take five years to complete. Then it would be necessary to go back to Congress for authority to make a detailed design and engineering study. That would take another five years. Only then could we seek formal project authorization.

That meant, I replied, that this project would still be in the talking stage ten years from now. Even were I to remain in office a full eight years (most Interior secretaries lasted less than four), through two presidential terms, we would have nothing to show but another stack of statistics and studies.

"Would it be possible to combine the feasibility and design studies on a single track? Could we compress the two into one five-year period?" I asked.

"That would be highly unusual," he replied. "But not impossible . . . provided the Congress is willing to authorize such a procedure."

I had difficulty reading his intent. Was he just trying to pass the buck and get out of this meeting without making any commitments? Or did he actually mean to be both helpful and at the same time realistic? We finally agreed to form a task force to examine the alternatives and report back to us within sixty days.

To my surprise, the task force came back on time and with a recommendation that the Corps support a congressional request for a foreshortened study process. By the end of 1993 we had obtained congressional authorization and funding, largely through the efforts of Senator Bob Graham, who had been a dedicated Everglades advocate ever since his days as governor of Florida. By remaining in the background, proceeding under the cover of a military organization, and asking for just a modest appropriation for yet another study, we had managed to begin work on a new vision of land management without attracting undue attention or overt opposition. And I was beginning to appreciate the value of this new partner: the Corps had credibility among conservatives most likely to be suspicious of anything that smacked of environmentalism.

We had a foot in the door and now had five years in which to shepherd the study along, all the while explaining the project to the local and national press and otherwise attempting to transform Everglades restoration into a visible national priority. In Florida, Governor Lawton Chiles provided strong support, notably by appointing a statewide study commission chaired by a remarkable former state legislator, Richard Pettigrew. Through unrelenting personal effort, Pettigrew managed to produce a unanimous vote from the one-hundred-member commission in favor of the state committing 50 percent of the restoration funding.

We also had five years in which to turn the Corps into a real believer and to keep it from backsliding as the study took shape. Somehow we had to imbue the study with a clear, uncompromising point of view that would, in turn, inform myriad decisions about reconfiguring the landscape and regulating the waters as they flowed through and around hundreds miles of canals and levees, locks and water-pumping stations.

The 1948 partition plan had proceeded from the top down, giving priority to expanding agriculture at the upper end of the watershed. Downstream uses were accommodated only to the extent they did not interfere with upstream agriculture. The only water reaching the Everglades at the terminus of the watershed was the residual left after satisfying the needs of agriculture and the cities. Our task for restoration was to proceed in the opposite order, from the bottom up, according priority to the needs of Everglades National Park, thereby upending the old "agriculture first" perspective. We would start with the question, "How much water is minimally necessary, at the right time and in the right places, to provide for the purposes of the park, to guarantee a functioning, sustainable ecosystem?"

How much water? Certainly we could not restore the Everglades to its original condition, when waters flowed unimpeded through the entire drainage from the small lakes on the outskirts of Orlando, down the Kissimmee River into Lake Okeechobee, overflowing and spreading to form a continuous river of grass that ultimately merged into the waters of Florida Bay. But to have any chance of saving the Everglades National Park ecosystem, scientists estimated that we would need to increase downstream flows by at least 50 percent.

WITH THE STUDY launched into its five-year orbit, we needed to retain public interest, political support, and congressional momentum for Everglades restoration. Fortunately, some Everglades-related issues required immediate legislation and appropriations. At the top of the list was water pollution from the sugar plantations.

The conflict with the sugar growers had begun more than a decade before my arrival in Washington. In the 1980s naturalists noticed an unusual change in the wetlands downstream of the sugar plantations: the normal dun-colored saw grass bordering the drainage canals was being replaced by brilliant green thickets that resembled the upstream fields of sugarcane. Wherever the irrigation drainage flowed, the green streaks followed. This new crop was not sugarcane, however, but common cattails, spreading in dense stands and driving out the saw grass, water lilies, and other plants endemic to the natural, low-nutrient waters of the Everglades.

Cattails had always been a minor part of the natural vegetation, occurring in small clusters beneath rookery trees where they were fertilized by bird droppings. But now they had become runaway invaders, forcing other plants aside and threatening to disrupt the entire ecological system. The cattails were transforming a complex wetland system into a simplified monoculture.

Scientists soon identified the cause—too much nutrient, not from bird droppings, but from the massive doses of phosphorus fertilizers used on the cane fields. The drainage water, saturated with dissolved phosphorus, was spreading out into the downstream wetlands and stimulating the growth of cattails.

The sugar companies were clearly responsible, and in 1989 federal prosecutors had filed suit against the state of Florida, asking that the court order the state to clean up the phosphorus pollution by enforcing clean-water regulations. The lawsuit awakened public interest and put the sugar companies in the public spotlight, igniting a debate about the relative values of heavily subsidized corporate agriculture versus the long-term integrity of the Everglades. The litigation dragged on incessantly, producing partial settlements that then spawned new lawsuits, inflaming emotions, consuming resources, and distracting everyone from the larger issue—restoration of the hydrologic functions of the Everglades system by providing more water and reconfiguring levees, canals, and roadways that blocked and disrupted water flows.

Once again, those of us seeking Everglades restoration had a choice. We could continue litigating against the sugar companies, spending years in the courts and in the process forfeiting any chance to build the public consensus necessary to sustain a comprehensive restoration program. Or we could settle. Time was the enemy. We chose to settle by agreeing on a phosphorus limit, setting a timetable, and apportioning the costs of compliance among the parties.

Settling the litigation meant bargaining with the devil. The sugar growers were led by a pair of Cuban expatriates, brothers Alfie and Pepe Fanjul. Within a decade after leaving Cuba, the Fanjuls had transplanted their plantation system to the Everglades and had become Florida's dominant sugar producers. Along the way, they had honed their political skills, befriending politicians with lavish political contributions, Alfie to Democrats and Pepe to Republicans.

To environmentalists the Fanjuls were the embodiment of what was wrong with Florida agriculture—too much money and political influence, pervasive labor violations, subsidies, and price supports that overcharged consumers, all topped off by widespread damage to the environment. American consumers were paying twice the international market price for sugar and the Everglades was being ruined, while poverty-stricken farmers throughout the Caribbean and Central America were denied access to American markets. The right approach to "big sugar," based on this view, would be simply to withdraw the egregious federal price supports, loan guarantees, and import quotas, stand by while the industry collapsed, and allow the plantation area to revert to natural wetlands, becoming once again an integral part of the Everglades system.

It was an appealing idea, but unlikely to happen on our watch. In the Congress, Democrats were as deeply complicit in protectionist farm policy as Republicans. Staking our restoration hopes on persuading Congress to end subsidies and thereby drive sugar out of the Everglades was no more practicable than continuing to litigate in the courts.

It was time to bargain. I invited Alfie Fanjul, the designated Democrat, to meet. We began by exchanging well-rehearsed, oft-repeated positions. Phosphorous, he explained, "is an essential element for all plant life. The Everglades is phosphorus-deficient. More phosphorus is good for the Everglades."

I countered by explaining that low phosphorous was precisely what made the Everglades such a distinctive landscape; the unique forms of plant life had evolved in response to the ultralow phosphorus content in the natural waters of the region. Restoring those conditions was essential to preserving the natural system.

As the discussion proceeded, it was clear that Fanjul had an impressive grasp of the issues; he spoke spontaneously, without deferring to his lawyers. Then he came to the point: the sugar growers were willing to negotiate but they could not afford to pay the entire cost of a cleanup. Besides, they were not the only polluters; there were also sod farms, vegetable growers, and alfalfa fields in the area, as well as small towns discharging treated sewage loaded with phosphorous and nitrogen nutrients. I conceded in turn that some portion of the cleanup should be paid from public funds; after all, it was the government that had established the Everglades Agricultural Area in the first place.

I agreed to negotiate. In the following weeks as we developed our position, I came to realize that there was a lot more at stake than just the restoration of the Everglades. Contaminated agricultural runoff was, and still is, the major unresolved water-quality problem in virtually every watershed in the country. In many of our rivers, lakes, and estuaries, water pollution from contaminated agricultural runoff has reached catastrophic proportions.

Given this history, any plan for the Everglades could become an important precedent, not only for other national parks, but for Chesapeake Bay, the Gulf of Mexico, and for rivers, lakes, and estuaries throughout the country. And if we could not deal convincingly with the land use issue here in the Everglades, where it threatened the destruction of a significant national park, what hope was there for rivers and water bodies in other parts of the country?

In the Everglades the phosphorus levels in the irrigation drainage water had soared to about two hundred parts per billion, more than twenty times the natural background level. The obvious solution was to regulate sugar growers and other farms to meet the ten parts per billion discharge standard recommended by scientists as necessary for protection of these waters. Under the complex provisions of the federal Clean Water Act, the state had to be a party to the agreement; that would require legislation, and to get action from the Florida legislature we had to demonstrate that requiring compliance would be economically feasible.

The first step in reducing phosphorous runoff was simply to use less fertilizer. Farmers, subjected to the aggressive sales tactics of the agricultural chemical industry, often use at least twice as much fertilizer as actually necessary for optimum production, leaving large quantities to wash from the land into nearby streams. Under pressure to reform, the sugar industry, by adopting best management practices, would quickly learn to cut fertilizer application by more than half, bringing phosphorous contamination levels below one hundred parts per billion.

In pollution control, the last increments of reduction are always the most difficult to accomplish and the sugar industry was no exception. Natural processes offered the best way to reduce remaining phosphorous levels. It had long since been demonstrated that farmers could reduce contaminated runoff by leaving natural buffers of trees and shrubs around their land to soak up and sequester the excess nutrients. The Everglades would be the place to translate this simple concept into an effective regulatory program.

Studying the specifics of the region, scientists came up with a "hair of the dog" solution. Since cattails were proliferating by absorbing the phosphorus from agricultural runoff, why not starve them out from the saw grass by planting buffer zones around the sugar fields, where artificial cattail planting could soak up and sequester contaminants before they reached the Everglades. Our engineers calculated that by dedicating about 4 percent of the sugar fields on the downstream side of the Everglades Agricultural Area to buffer zones planted thick with cattails, the resulting filtered runoff would emerge close to the ten parts per billion water standard. The optimum design called for four large artificial cattail swamps, designated as "stormwater treatment areas," each about ten thousand acres in size, through which all irrigation runoff could be slowly drained and filtered.

With a workable plan, and agreement on cost sharing among the state, the federal government, and the sugar growers led by the Fanjuls, we announced the outlines of a settlement. Not everyone was happy. Environmental leaders showed up to assure the press that we had sold them out, undercutting their efforts to make the industry pay for every last cent of cleanup costs that would eventually mount to more than five hundred million dollars. It made little difference that Senator Bob Graham, who in his long political career had done more than any other individual on behalf of the Everglades, was in attendance to endorse the settlement.

We then converged upon Tallahassee to ask the Florida legislature to enact the plan into law. The sugar industry, sourly reconciled to settlement as the better alternative to the risks of continued litigation, reluctantly lobbied for our proposal. The legislature, astonished by longtime adversaries in at least temporary agreement, in the spring of 1994 passed the Everglades Forever Act, setting mandatory water-quality standards, apportioning costs, and establishing a compliance deadline of 2006.

Within a year of construction, the cattail swamps had vindicated our approach. Beyond the banks of the impoundments the solid masses of cattails blended nicely with the surrounding cane fields — one monoculture designed to mitigate the other. Swarms of waterfowl began to circle over the cattail swamps, landing and feeding in the openings. Duck hunters soon followed, creating yet another constituency for Everglades restoration.

BEYOND AGRICULTURAL POLLUTION, the other urgent, not to be deferred issue in the Everglades was land use regulation. Developers were invading faster than cattails. In the years following World War II, Miami, Fort Lauderdale, West Palm Beach, Hillsborough, and the other Atlantic coastal communities had expanded rapidly, gradually merging into one another to form a hundred-mile-long urban strip. As the open spaces along the coast filled in, developers began looking westward toward the Everglades.

The logical boundary line that should have contained westward sprawl was the coastal levee, a long north-south flood-control structure paralleling the coastline about twenty miles inland. Florida promoters, however, have seldom allowed a line on a map to deter them from selling swampland to gullible investors. In the 1960s subdividers swarmed across the levee and began nationwide advertising and sales campaigns, inducing thousands of retirees to sign time-payment purchase contracts for Florida land they had never seen.

Now we were all stuck with the consequences: thousands of lots on the wrong side of the levee where defrauded buyers were trying to salvage their investments by clamoring for more flood-control dikes to divert the sheet flows still farther to the west, away from their land. More dikes would be disastrous for the Everglades, however, cutting off a downstream area called Taylor Slough, already short of water, from its remaining upstream sources.

The only way to save Taylor Slough was to draw a clear "thou shalt not develop" line along the coastal dike and then offer to buy out those who had already purchased land west of the dike. By 1999, with funding from Congress, the Park Service had managed to purchase or condemn more than two thousand swampland lots for inclusion within expanded park boundaries. Where lot buyers had ignored flood warnings and built in violation of (poorly enforced) building codes, the process of purchasing and retiring the land had stalled, with some holdouts demanding that the Corps spend millions on flood control rather than simply paying them fair compensation to remedy past mistakes. Nonetheless, by 2000 we had managed to shore up the Atlantic dike as a durable urban growth boundary, although not without continuing skirmishes between developers and county zoning commissions.

If the Everglades ecosystem was the obvious beneficiary of this urban growth boundary, so too were the cities and towns along Florida's Atlantic coast. With little room to expand outward, and bounded to the east by the ocean, communities now had to turn inward. Developers began taking a second look, reconsidering the vacant and underdeveloped urban spaces they had leapfrogged in the race toward and beyond the suburban fringe.

Urbanists have coined the phrase "eastward ho" to describe the process of infill and redevelopment now underway. West Palm Beach has become a center of the new urbanism, developing mixed-use, pedestrian-oriented projects. The seedy old downtown of Fort Lauderdale is coming alive with restaurants and retail and condominiums. As infill accelerates, the prospects for mass transit also increase.

The evolution of an urban boundary along coastal Florida, made possible by the unique topography, the requisites of flood control, and the proximity of the Everglades, has not been widely replicated.

Sprawl is hard to control; as cities grow, the centrifugal forces of development simply seem to accelerate, consuming more and more land on the perimeters. Between 1970 and 1990, the developed land area of metropolitan Los Angeles expanded by 300 percent while the population increased by 45 percent. In the same period the developed land area of metropolitan Chicago expanded by 49 percent while the population increased by 4 percent.

Typically the pressure to establish growth boundaries arises from inside a city as it struggles with infrastructure costs, traffic jams, air pollution, and a declining tax base. Yet most attempts to draw growth boundaries based on purely internal urban considerations have, with some exceptions in California and Oregon, failed in the face of intense opposition from the real-estate industry. South Florida is an instructive contrast because the urban growth boundary—the coastal dike—took shape outside the urban areas and was grounded in the need for flood control, subsequently strengthened by growing recognition that the ecological values of the Everglades ecosystem itself should be preserved.

The process of establishing an urban growth boundary, we learned, was better approached without an injunction to "stop right now." Instead, advocates should, like a general on the eve of battle, examine the maps, look carefully at the topography, the mountains and rivers and valleys, and then choose a strategic defensive line across the natural landscape, located a suitable distance beyond the existing development edge where escalating land values and development pressures have not yet drawn landowners into high-profile political battles over development rights. How to generalize the south Florida result to other metropolitan areas, less susceptible to flood disasters and without the proximity of a great national park, is a question we will return to in subsequent chapters.

As AGRICULTURAL RUNOFF was cleaned up and urban growth near the Everglades was contained, many issues remained. In 1998, with just two years left in President Clinton's second and last term, the Army Corps of Engineers finally completed the restoration study — the five-year planning process for a complete redesign and replumbing of the Everglades system that Congress had authorized back in 1993. Much had changed in that time. Republicans had taken control of both houses of Congress. The leadership of the Senate had turned over twice, as had that of the House. There had also been continual turnover within the Corps. By now we had worked with three successive commanding generals and three different district engineers in Florida, all the while laboring to keep the project afloat with annual appropriations and to keep the Corps focused on the restoration objective, even as the sugar industry and land developers tried to tilt the outcome in their respective directions.

Nonetheless the Corps proposal was a showstopper. It called for a thirty-year restoration program, at an estimated cost of eight billion dollars. The Corps has always been a proficient earthmover, and in the study the agency had now caught the spirit of moving the earth back to its original shape by erasing many earthworks that had accumulated over the years. The Corps proposed filling in fifteen hundred miles of drainage canals to retain water within the system and tearing out two hundred miles of dikes to allow water to spread evenly across the land. To allow water to flow unconstricted across critical sections of the Everglades, the plan called for rebuilding and elevating miles of roads and causeways onto pilings above the water. And it proposed purchasing additional lands for buffer zones along the east side of the coastal dike to prevent settlements whose demands would draw down water levels on the Everglades side.

In reviewing the study, we in Interior were less satisfied with those sections that proposed how to acquire and store more water on the land. The Corps had laid out plans to recapture and use much of the water that had been draining out of the system, running out to sea as agricultural drainage, stormwater runoff, and urban wastewater. But then came the difficult question: where to store all this recaptured water? In south Florida, the highest point on the land, excepting mounds of trash in landfills, is less than twenty feet above sea level. There are no river valleys where dams can be built to hold water. The only place to store water is on the land itself in huge shallow impoundments that mimic the way water was naturally stored in the presettlement Everglades. More surface storage would mean buying still more sugar plantations for conversion to wetlands.

The Corps was just not willing to risk any more political controversy over additional land acquisition. Without more land, though, the only alternative was to store the water underground by injecting it into the deep aquifers around Lake Okeechobee. Never shy about spending money to circumvent controversy, the Corps proposed constructing, at a cost of nearly two billion dollars, five hundred large injection wells to store water underground, from where it could be pumped back out and delivered onto the land in times of drought.

There was no need for such an expensive technological solution in our view. The better solution was simply to buy out enough of the remaining sugar farms to restore the original wetland flowways all the way to the south shore of Lake Okeechobee. These sugar farms were nearing the end of their productive lives anyway.

At Crewston, a tiny sugar town south of Lake Okeechobee, there is a white concrete column on which a red stripe has been painted at ground level each year since the surrounding sugar plantations went into production. The top stripe is now twelve feet above the ground, testimony to continuing disappearance of the shallow peat soils. Those soils, formed over millennia as plant material accumulated beneath the water, do not stay put when dried and exposed to air. They oxidize, crumbling to dust that gradually blows away. In another twenty to thirty years, the soils in much of the Everglades Agricultural Area will erode all the way down to limestone bedrock, where even price supports and quotas will not be enough to sustain the industry. Thus it may well be that by the time the injection well project is under way, the sugar growers will be the ones lobbying for the government to take the land off their hands and return it to wetlands.

Today, in 2005, injection wells remain part of the officially approved restoration plan, though sufficiently far down on the priority list that work has not commenced. Meanwhile a review committee of the National Academy of Sciences has expressed skepticism about the plan and has urged consideration of expanded surface storage. And a new generation of Everglades advocates has renewed old proposals to buy out all the remaining sugar plantations, or at least to purchase the development rights so that the depleted sugar lands do not become subdivisions that would pose an even larger pollution threat to the Everglades.

After our review of the Corps proposal, it was April 2000, and time was running out for us in the administration. The president was a lame duck and the chances for passing any further Everglades legislation, enacting the Corps restoration plan into law, seemed remote. But by June, I realized that I had again underestimated our chances of success. I had overlooked the upcoming presidential election. Florida with its twenty-six electoral votes had emerged as a swing state, one that might well determine the next president. And our eight years of unrelenting effort had transformed the Everglades into a front-page political issue that could affect the outcome.

I should have been quicker to comprehend the possibilities. We had been through this once before, back in 1996 when Bob Dole, then Senate majority leader, was running for president. Dole was a part-time Florida resident who spent the winter congressional breaks at his condominium in Bal Harbour, and he understood the voter appeal of Everglades issues.

Dole had spotted his chance for a grand gesture as the 1995 agricultural appropriations bill was readied for a final Senate vote. At the last minute, out of nowhere, without hearings or discussion, two hundred million dollars earmarked for Everglades land acquisition suddenly appeared in the bill. After the bill passed, I joined with Republican leaders in the Senate press room to lavish praise upon Senator Dole, took the check, and used it to purchase a large sugar plantation, the Talisman Farms, to be taken out of production and dedicated to water storage. The Republicans had learned how to do Everglades politics, not enough for Dole to carry Florida that year, but in the next presidential cycle in 2000 they would be back to write a different ending.

In June 2000 our Everglades restoration bill passed through the Senate Environment and Public Works Committee and then out of the Senate. In November the bill passed the House and went back to the Senate for final passage by a vote of 85 to 1. As we celebrated, confident that victory would boost Al Gore's election chances in Florida, I looked back uneasily at south Miami-Dade where the ghost of Hurricane Andrew still swirled over local politics.

The fate of the Homestead Air Force Base had still not been resolved, although from all appearances the Air Force was still on track to hand it over to the Cuban American jetport developers. Environmentalists, however, had not forgotten the Homestead deal making that took place back in 1993 in the wake of Hurricane Andrew. They now saw their own political opportunity and demanded that candidate Gore publicly declare his intention to kill the project.

Gore was in a tough spot. The Cuban community was still seething over Janet Reno's decision to send Elian Gonzalez, the eight-year-old boat refugee rescued from the Atlantic, back into the outstretched arms of Fidel Castro. The streets of Little Havana in south Miami were plastered with photographs of the terrified child being seized at gunpoint by federal agents.

Trapped between two critical constituencies, the Cuban community and environmental supporters, Gore remained painfully silent, hoping environmentalists would understand his dilemma and recognize that he would do after the election what he could not do before then—announce cancellation of the jetport project. To underscore the obvious, I spoke in opposition to the jetport. Carol Browner, the Environmental Protection Agency administrator, did the same.

But the situation only got worse. Vocal Cuban Americans continued to remind Gore of President Clinton's promise of support. Infuriated environmentalists refused to accept our assurances that Gore would do the right thing if elected. Bill Bradley, campaigning in the Democratic primaries, challenged Gore to denounce the jetport plan. Then Ralph Nader piled on, making the same demand as the general election neared. On November 4, Nader and his Green Party received nearly one hundred thousand votes, votes that, like butterfly ballots, Elian, and the Supreme Court, determined the outcome of the closest presidential race in American history.

In hindsight, with a keener appreciation of Florida history, we might have avoided the trap. Our response to Hurricane Andrew back in 1993 had been to defer to local officials and look the other way while the political deals were cut. It had been all too easy to accept the slogan "land use planning is a local matter," even when the land at issue was a federal facility sitting on environmentally sensitive lands smack between two national parks. And, predictably, once the election was over, we persuaded the president to scrap the jetport plan.

In early December 2000 we gathered in the Oval Office to watch as President Clinton signed the Everglades restoration legislation into law. It was not much of a celebration. The Supreme Court was that very morning hearing final arguments preparatory to awarding Florida's electoral votes to George W. Bush. The president made only a few perfunctory remarks, and then we drifted away. Outside the West Wing I spoke briefly to the press, made small talk with

Florida governor Jeb Bush, and left, reflecting not about the future, but on what we had accomplished in the past eight years. There was no question that Everglades restoration was the most important legislative accomplishment for the environment during the Clinton administration. For the previous eight years, Congress had refused to act on major environmental proposals, and we had spent most of our time on Capitol Hill defending existing laws from repeated efforts to weaken them. And again I wondered, how had we managed to push through an eight-billion-dollar restoration program that would fundamentally alter the allocation of land and water resources away from further development and back toward natural systems? Why such a spectacular success in the Everglades in a time of failures elsewhere? And what were the lessons for the future in other parts of the country?

The simple answer is that the Everglades success was an aberration, a case of being in the right place when it came time to make a down payment on a presidential election. But in truth the answer is more complex, and it is rooted in the changing nature of conservation politics and the process of enacting environmental legislation.

Back in the 1960s and '70s, when environmental concerns came to the national stage, Congress enacted broad, comprehensive laws, including the National Environmental Policy Act, the Wilderness Act, the Clean Air and Clean Water acts, and the Endangered Species Act, to name a few. Since that time the environment has faded somewhat as a political issue, and since 2000 the Bush administration has set out to destroy the bipartisan consensus that produced these laws.

Notwithstanding these attempts, the public health issues relating to pollution control, the so-called brown issues that fall largely within the jurisdiction of the Environmental Protection Agency, continue to attract national attention and debate. Voters no matter where they live share common fears about breathing sulfur dioxide from power plants, eating fish contaminated with mercury, or drinking water contaminated by cryptosporidium, and they will continue to demand national measures to assure clean air and clean drinking water.

In contrast the Bush administration has done much more damage to the so-called green issues, those relating to land conservation and restoration, precisely because these are typically characterized as local issues. Overgrazing in Arizona is not of much interest to citizens of Maine and the decline of Atlantic salmon is not a big issue in Texas. Yet without federal leadership, our river basins and regional landscapes will continue to degrade. And if there is an urgent lesson to be derived from the Florida Everglades, it is that we must invent new federal-state partnerships for managing and restoring our lands, partnerships that have sufficient charisma and public support to withstand destructive efforts by later administrations.

Which leads us back to the central question posed above: could the Everglades effort mark the beginning of a national commitment to large-scale restoration of degraded ecosystems? Or is it an aberration, a one-time event, of historic significance as yet another example of directions not taken in our episodic, faltering quest for an appropriate national role in land use planning?

It is easy to think of the Everglades consensus as a one time occurrence — something of a perfect storm spawned by a unique mix of killer hurricanes and floods ravaging a defenseless landscape, intensified by national concern for a world-renowned, highly vulnerable national park and abetted by exceptional personalities and closely contested presidential elections. But there is another way to conceptualize the Everglades experience, one that provides an instructive precedent for large-scale land use planning and restoration efforts in other regions of the country.

The opportunities become visible when we reduce the Everglades experience, in all its biological and political complexities, to its two most essential characteristics: first, the Everglades can be seen as a river system not that different from the rivers in other parts of the country; and second, the indispensable federal actor is the Army Corps of Engineers, which is primarily responsible for flood control on virtually every river in America and by that fact the most important of all federal land management agencies.

PEELING AWAY THE LAYERS of semitropical biology, the Everglades at its core is just another river system, prone to severe flooding, which over time proved to be a death warrant as settlers moved in, appropriating lands in the natural floodplains only to demand federal help when the inevitable flood disasters followed. Drainage and levee projects followed, opening still more land for development. The flood cycle repeated and the Corps responded with still more projects to diminish and control the river. Settlers and the government became locked into a constantly escalating struggle to reduce the river to drainage canals. Eventually, the natural river system and its riparian habitat and wildlife became so disrupted and degraded that entire ecological systems began to collapse. This describes not just the Everglades, but an historic sequence that has taken place on most rivers in the United States.

In my first year as secretary of the interior I encountered another event that seemed at first to have all the necessary ingredients of a large-scale Everglades-style restoration opportunity, something that would demonstrate how the emerging federal-state partnership for Everglades restoration could be applied in other parts of the country. The occasion was yet another flood disaster. The rains began in April in the upper Midwest. In mid-May, water levels began to rise on both the Missouri and the Mississippi rivers, and by early summer more than five million acres of farmland were under water in Nebraska, Iowa, Missouri, and Illinois.

It was the worst flood in the Mississippi River basin since the great disaster of 1927, when the lower Mississippi broke through the levees, inundating nearly twenty million acres in the Delta

region of Arkansas, Mississippi, and Louisiana. After two trips
to the Midwest to survey the damage, President Clinton issued
disaster declarations and then appointed a review committee, led
by a retired Corps commander, Brigadier General Gerald Galloway
Jr., to assess the situation and recommend changes in management
of the rivers. It was not difficult to spot parallels to the Everglades
experience. In response to the great disaster of 1927, Congress
had put the Corps in charge of flood-control planning on the
Mississippi, setting a precedent for dispatching the Corps to Florida
in wake of the Lake Okeechobee hurricane disaster of 1928.
And if my theory that flood disasters can set the stage for land
use change held water, well, here was a promising opportunity
to effect change in the largest watershed of all—the Missouri-
Mississippi, which covers parts of thirty-two states from western
New York to western Montana and from eastern Tennessee to central Colorado.

In the following months the Galloway committee examined the
hydrologic history of the basin and the storm sequences that
resulted in flooding, and the committee made many technical recommendations for improving river management and the accuracy
of flood forecasting. It also concluded that, as in Florida, years of
flood-control projects had effectively destroyed the natural character of the once-lush river valleys by the building of huge levees close
to the water, which in turn promoted the destruction of the rich bottomland forests as they were converted to farmland.

The Galloway committee determined that the elimination of
natural floodplains by levee construction had in some instances
actually served to increase the threat of flood damage. The committee concluded that "where significant wetlands exist, they can have
a noticeable effect on discharge peaks from the basin," meaning
simply that if flood surges have more room to spread out across the
natural river bottoms, less water will move toward downstream
communities.

With these committee conclusions I began to comprehend an opportunity for change in the Missouri-Mississippi watershed. The Galloway report, comparable in a general way to the Corps study that would later trigger congressional authorization of Everglades restoration, could be the springboard for an analogous program in the largest of our river systems. I then set out to sell the idea.

At the University of Wisconsin I described the findings of the Galloway committee and explained that the flood-control projects along the river had made for larger floods by destroying floodplains and by imprisoning the rivers tightly between artificial levees. Some hydrologists estimated that if just half the original wetlands in the upper Midwest had remained in place, they could have soaked up and held all of the 1993 floodwaters. Instead of simply replacing the ruptured and damaged levees, I suggested, why not remove the levees, allowing the rivers to move naturally in their floodplains, in the process regenerating the backwaters and hardwood forests that had once covered the river bottoms.

My audiences were not enthusiastic, in Wisconsin or elsewhere. Was I proposing that all levee systems be removed? No, I acknowledged, there are some areas, particularly in the Mississippi Delta region where the river valleys are so flat and shallow that in the absence of levees a large flood, such as occurred in 1927, could spill outward across the land for tens or hundreds of miles. In the upper river basin, above St. Louis, however, the rivers generally run in relatively narrow valleys that provide natural and relatively confined limits to flooding. In many of these areas levees are not really necessary, another example of the tendency of the Corps to build projects just to keep busy and to justify larger appropriation requests.

Most of the groups I met were interested in not less but more development, particularly of the Mississippi. In Illinois, Iowa, and Minnesota, grain buyers wanted the Corps to build even larger barge locks on the Mississippi, permanently flooding more forests in order to speed barge traffic through the locks. All along the river, farmers questioned taking even a few acres of land protected by the levees out of production.

These objections sounded quite familiar to what we were hearing from sugar growers in Florida. The difference here, however, was the virtual absence of public support for change. There were few environmental organizations calling for river restoration, the regional press seemed lethargic, and members of Congress, sensing no public demand, made clear they would protect the status quo. And the Corps, so helpful in Florida, was nowhere to be seen advocating restoration; in fact the agency was still promoting projects for more land clearing in Mississippi and for dredging yet another river in Arkansas. This was definitely not Florida.

As the Galloway report began to gather dust, I reflected on other lessons learned. The most important was scale. The Mississippi-Missouri system was simply too large and complex a place to begin. In Florida we were dealing with a single state, one region of which, the Everglades, had garnered national attention only after decades of grassroots advocacy and attention by the press. On the Mississippi, we were too soon on too large a stage.

EVEN AS THE PROSPECTS for change in the heartland faded, another flood and drought cycle, this time in California, provided what would be one last chance during the Clinton administration to replicate the essential elements of the Everglades experience in the form of a federal-state partnership for regional water management and ecosystem restoration. This time the impetus for reform came from a statewide drought beginning in the 1980s that had diminished the Sierra Nevada snowpack and reduced runoff in the Sacramento and other rivers in the Central Valley, threatening a reduction of water supplies to valley farms and cities. Then a small fish called the delta smelt, which spawns in the river delta at the head of San Francisco Bay, was threatened with extinction because of inadequate freshwater flows into the bay and was placed on the endangered species list.

Angered by the listing, Governor Pete Wilson vowed that water deliveries from upstream reservoirs would never be diverted from farms just to protect a fish that only a few biologists and fishers had ever heard of. The federal Fish and Wildlife Service, with my support, held firm, and in January 1994 the pumps at Tracy, which draw water from the delta into canals for delivery to farms and cities to the south, were temporarily shut down to maintain downstream flows at a critical moment in the spawning cycle of the fish. Suddenly the delta smelt was on the front pages, and California headed toward another epic struggle over water.

After some preliminary skirmishing, I met in Sacramento with Governor Wilson, and we agreed to convene statewide negotiations on California's water future. Meanwhile Fish and Wildlife, given some regulatory space by a year of high rainfall, was able to assure full deliveries to farmers without affecting the fisheries. Lengthy negotiations ensued as the number of stakeholders grew ever larger, drawing in all water users with an interest in the rivers that drain from the Sierra Nevada into San Francisco Bay, including agriculture, conservationists, the Metropolitan Water District, San Francisco and other Bay Area cities, interested legislators and congressional staffers, and representatives from federal agencies, including the Bureau of Reclamation and the ever-present Army Corps of Engineers.

The negotiations dragged on, interrupted by a turnover from the Republican Wilson administration to a Democratic governor, Gray Davis. Finally, in August 2000, we signed a comprehensive agreement outlining a thirty-year program, at an estimated cost of some twenty billion dollars, to restructure the river and canal systems of central California, from Mount Shasta in the north, along the Sacramento River, and south across the mountains to Los Angeles. Californians, numbering more than thirty-five million, had finally come to appreciate that they could not go on using water by drying up rivers, and destroying fish populations.

The program calls for dismantling several small dams that block fish passage, increasing the storage capacity of existing dams rather than building new dams on virgin sites, moving levees to restore river floodplains, and providing legal assurance for minimum river flows to guarantee fish passage and to protect the extensive wetlands in the bay delta. Along the way, the program picked up the less than evocative title "CalFed," a name more appropriate for a savings and loan than for the most far-reaching land and water management program in California history. In 2004, three years after the Clinton administration left office, a united California delegation managed to push the program to approval in Congress.

Looking back on the California experience, I could see its clear relation to what was happening in a parallel time frame in Florida at the other end of the country. In both cases extreme natural events—somewhat different cycles of hurricanes, flooding, and drought—had eventually brought the public face-to-face with the limits imposed by their natural environment. And in both cases circumstances had forced the question of whether to forge ahead in the name of progress, depleting and destroying the surrounding ecosystems, or to set a new course toward a sustainable future.

THE SUCCESSES in Florida and California, contrasted with failure in the Mississippi River basin, educated me to the enormous political obstacles inherent in multistate river restoration planning, which would have to await another time. And in California I finally came to understand the split personality of the Army Corps of Engineers, so helpful in Florida and California and so obstinately uncooperative in the Midwest.

Corps projects do not flow from policy set by the executive branch in Washington; they reflect the priorities of individual members of Congress carried out through the classic log-rolling process

within appropriations committees. If local voters want to transform their presumptive share of congressional largesse from "flood
control" to river restoration, and if their member of Congress hears
that message, there will be no opposition in Washington. It is only a
matter of getting in line and waiting until your turn comes. The
budget of the Corps reflects, not a national policy, but the aggregate
sum of what individual members of Congress want. That is the
most basic, and consistent, lesson from the Florida Everglades, the
Midwest, and California.

Leaving office in 2001, I was not satisfied that we had learned all
we could from our failure with the two-thirds of the country within
the Mississippi-Missouri watershed. In the fall of 2002 I found
myself traveling from St. Louis to Phoenix, and as we left Lambert
Field and gained cruising altitude I looked out the window as
the rising sun cast the landscape into sharp relief. I followed the
Missouri River as it made a wide northern loop around St. Louis
and then traced it west across Missouri to the Kansas border
where it finally turned north, gradually dissolving into the mid-
morning haze.

Viewed from thirty thousand feet, the river floodplain is a distinct, shallow trough, perhaps five miles wide, that cuts straight and
clean across the hilly farm country that rises on both sides. Within
that floodplain the silvery river strand snakes from one side of the
plain to the other. But it is a dead snake, rigid, unable to move, con-
stricted by the levees along its banks. The side channels and floodplain forests are long gone, replaced by treeless expanses of corn
and soybeans.

The dredging and channeling of the lower Missouri proved to be
another Corps fiasco. Midwestern farmers already had access to the
entire length of the Mississippi, to railroads, and to interstate highways to transport their grain. They had no need for a barge channel,
and it has gone largely unused.

From this altitude it was not difficult to imagine the bottomland forests that once wrapped an emerald ribbon all the way across Missouri, sheltering and feeding vast flocks of ducks, geese, sand-hill cranes, plovers, and songbirds. And it was easy to visualize restoring the forests by simply removing the levees and allowing the river to reclaim its floodplain, letting it meander back and forth between the natural levees of the surrounding hilly uplands.

The passenger seated next to me eventually asked what there could possibly be down below that I found so interesting. I explained, and suggested, "The entire river corridor from St. Louis to Kansas City should be a national park. Imagine re-creating the river that Lewis and Clark saw when they set out from St. Louis to discover and lay claim to a continent."

"But what about the towns along the river?" he responded.

"Look down there," I replied. "There aren't very many. They are small towns that faded when the steamboats gave way to the rail-roads that went north and south of the river. They have a lot of his-tory, they would remain, and they could generate more income from being near a national park than from growing surplus crops."

By then I was losing my audience; he went back to the *Wall Street Journal*, and I began thinking of the failed aftermath of the Galloway report. We had bitten off way too much, but here in front of me, or more accurately down below, was what we should have con-centrated on. A one-state project—the three-hundred-mile river length across Missouri from St. Louis to Kansas City. A river stretch with natural floodplain limits. A river that had been dredged and leveed to create a barge channel for which the traffic never devel-oped. And then I recalled that we had actually done a demonstration project in the wake of the 1993 Mississippi flood.

In this three-hundred-mile stretch across central Missouri, the river had breached the levees and waters had overflowed much of the natural floodplain. As the floodwaters receded, the corn and soybean farms along the river emerged heavily scoured, smothered in banks of mud and sand and covered with rafts of uprooted trees and driftwood. Near the town of Columbia, floodplain farms were so badly damaged that the owners were ready to give up the struggle and cash out rather than rebuild levees and clear the land once again.

At our urging, Congress appropriated sufficient funds to purchase and retire five thousand acres of farmland to demonstrate how a restoration program might work. Today, less than fifteen years later, the riverbanks are crowded with shoulder-high thickets of cottonwood and willow. Flocks of ducks and geese feed in the river's meandering side channels. The Big Muddy National Wildlife Refuge is a preview of what the future could be all along the lower Missouri.

My thoughts began to turn as the plane neared Phoenix—time to move on to other matters. But elsewhere out on the land, I felt certain, the Everglades example would inspire citizens to look afresh at their rivers and wetlands, to imagine what once was and could again be.

2

Cities in
the Wilderness

AS THE FIRST Clinton administration settled into Washington and began discussing priorities, I soon discovered that for the near term I would be contending with issues left unresolved by my predecessors, beginning with an endangered bird, the northern spotted owl. Some months previously, a federal judge in Seattle had taken the unprecedented step of halting timber sales in national forests in the Pacific Northwest to protect the owl.

With these forests off-limits, the timber industry up in arms, laid-off loggers picketing in the streets, and mill owners running low on inventory, something had to give, and there were just two possibilities: our administration could devise a forest plan acceptable to the judge or the Congress would intervene to exempt the owl from the provisions of the Endangered Species Act. It made little difference that our predecessors had created the crisis by their obdurate refusal to comply with the plain requirements of the act (inside the Beltway what happened yesterday is ancient history); the campaign was over and it was now our problem.

In April the president convened a town-hall meeting in Portland, inviting participants to discuss how to strike a balance between protecting the owl and letting loggers back into the forests. It was a vintage Clinton performance; for a full day we sat around a table sweltering beneath klieg lights and cameras while he listened thoughtfully and asked insightful questions in response to presentations from elected officials, labor leaders, mill owners, scientists, conservationists, civic representatives, and the bishop of Portland. The only light moments came from the proprietor of the Blue Ox Millworks.

The Blue Ox, it turned out, was a one-man, two-ox operation in the redwood forests of Northern California. The Blue Ox, the owner explained, obtained its inventory without cutting any green trees at all. Instead it used teams of oxen to salvage dead and down redwood trees, hauling them out without roads or otherwise scarring the surrounding forests. Nice idea, I thought, but not quite sufficient to revive a regional timber industry. It reminded me of when a candidate in the 1988 presidential campaign had suggested that Iowa farmers, under stress from falling corn and soybean prices, might make a better living growing Belgian endive.

At the end of the long day, the president left town, leaving us behind to contend with the heightened expectations on all sides of the controversy. I began commuting to the Pacific Northwest in search of solutions, trekking through old-growth stands, helicoptering up to view the patterns of forest destruction caused by clear-cutting—and by the recent eruption of Mount St. Helens— and sighting several owls. What I saw everywhere was bewildering complexity; every time I began to grasp a bit of knowledge, it seemed to slide away into a maze of intertwined factors affecting the forest in some other way. The owl, I discovered, was just one link in a complicated food chain of predators and prey. Even the owl was not entirely safe from predation; it needed the canopy cover of the large trees to protect it from hawks as it skimmed through the forests. In the forests it fed mainly on flying squirrels, which in turn fed on fungi that grew on rotting logs on the forest floor. Would even the Blue Ox Mill, I wondered, threaten the owl's survival by removing the logs that grew the fungi that fed the squirrel that nourished the owl?

In the streams, I observed the first spawning coho salmon that I had ever seen—and soon learned that they were as dependent on the forest as the owl. The dense forest growth overhanging the streams shaded and cooled the waters and provided mountainside cover that filtered sediment from runoff; dead and down material from the forest attracted insects, which in turn became food for the fish. The lines spread outward into hundreds of species and thousands of linkages.

Through this fog of biological complexity one fact was becoming clear. Before we could get to a decision about how much forest to protect in order to assure survival of the owl and other forest-dependent species, we would have to learn a lot more about how the parts of the forest functioned as a whole. And that meant we needed much more scientific information about the entire forest ecosystem. The president's public commitment to finding a solution guaranteed the necessary resources, so we began putting teams of scientists on the ground and in the laboratories of the Northwest. More than two hundred geologists, biologists, land planners, hydrologists, zoologists, and other specialists began to assemble the necessary information with which to develop a plan.

AS THE SCIENCE TEAMS went to work, I began to think about the broader political significance of what was happening. This was the first time that anyone had approached an endangered species controversy by proposing to get the science right—at least on such a grand scale. Whatever decisions lay down the road, we would begin by calling a time out, herding the political players off the field and bringing in the scientists to gather the data and produce an unimpeachable scientific consensus for what it would take to preserve this forest ecosystem. When the science report came back, the politicians would once again take the field but no one could contend we had not used "good science," a complaint that had become a common refrain among critics of the Endangered Species Act.

Strong science is essential to administering the Endangered Species Act in at least two ways. The first comes in the initial process of "listing," determining the population numbers below which a species is likely to become extinct. The second determination, equally complex, is to assess how much habitat, whether old-growth forests, wetlands, or native prairie, must be preserved or restored to sustain a population large enough to assure species survival. Why not, I wondered, make such scientific research part of solving disputes under the act, not just in the Northwest but in every case where a species appeared to be in decline or in danger of extinction? Rather than just "reviewing the literature" prior to making a regulatory decision, government agencies should affirmatively develop better research and information.

Congress frequently turns to the National Academy of Sciences for advice on science issues, and that seemed the logical place both to seek guidance and to widen the circle of consensus for legislation. The academy responded by assembling a panel of scientists, led by Peter Raven, the renowned director of the Missouri Botanical Garden, to examine the concept. The panel met for several months and returned with a persuasive report explaining the importance of a government-led effort to inventory and understand the biological resources of our country. "The United States," the report concluded, "is committed to attempting to preserve its biological heritage. Fulfilling those commitments requires accurate and extensive information on the evolutionary relationships among species, their biology and the status and trends of their distribution and abundance."

There was, moreover, ample precedent for gathering such information. Thomas Jefferson, in his instructions to Meriwether Lewis, dated June 20, 1803, had commanded him to take note of new species, including "the dates at which particular plants put forth or lose their flower, or leaf, times of appearance of particular birds, reptiles, or insects."

The concept of an institutional "biological survey" seemed especially appropriate, one for which there was an illuminating historical precedent: the United States Geological Survey. Established in 1879, the USGS has for more than a century served the nation by mapping and investigating our mineral resources and by monitoring our rivers and other water resources, providing a useful and widely accepted basis for sensible land use planning. Placing biology on a plane with geology and water would be a logical, and long overdue, progression, destined to prove just as useful in the management of our natural resources.

Supplied with these arguments and the Academy of Sciences report, we took our case for the legislation to Capitol Hill. In the House, Gerry Studds, chairman of the committee with jurisdiction over endangered species issues, responded enthusiastically and agreed to sponsor a bill based on the academy recommendations. Sid Yates, the influential chair of the Interior appropriations committee, added his support. It was, he told me, the most important new earth science initiative since Congress had sponsored and funded the International Geophysical Year back in 1959.

In the summer of 1993 the bill came to the House floor for debate, the first piece of environmental legislation to reach the floor in the new Congress, and therefore something of a bellwether for upcoming environmental initiatives. Democrats were still in control of Congress and the prospects for passage seemed good — until the debate got under way. I soon learned that we had completely misjudged the temper of this new Congress.

Opponents, Republicans and Democrats, assailed the bill as a threat to the property rights of every American. More knowledge of what is out on the land, they argued, would lead to the discovery of more endangered species and that would mean regulation of land use, limiting owners' rights to use land as they see fit.

I suggested that the opposite was more likely; if we could identify the problems with potentially endangered species before they reached the crisis point, scientific understanding would give us more time and a lot more flexibility in working out solutions that could accommodate both landowner expectations and the requirements of the Endangered Species Act. We also needed this broader biological information in order to make good decisions about use of the land — where to locate highways, port facilities, airports, utility corridors, power plants, military bases, subdivisions, and shopping centers without unnecessarily disrupting the natural systems that sustain us.

Unpersuaded, our opponents broadened the attack: "Land use planning," they argued, "is a local matter." The federal government, they claimed, had never been involved in land use policy, and this was no time to begin.

American history, however, tells a very different story. The federal government has always been involved in land use planning, going clear back to George Washington's proposals to improve navigation on the Potomac River, not incidentally to open the way for development of his land claims along the Kanawha River in West Virginia. And as the nation moved west, Congress sent army engineers to survey and stake out transcontinental railroad routes, which the federal government then subsidized with generous land grants. To this day the Army Corps of Engineers serves as an engineering and construction company, dedicated to opening lands for development by planning and building flood-control projects throughout the nation. And in arid regions where there is not enough water, another agency, the Bureau of Reclamation, dams the rivers to divert the waters to subsidize more growth and development. And then there is the land use planning embodied in the interstate highway program under which the federal government has funded and directed national development with a network of more than forty thousand miles of highways.

Land use planning has thus been a federal function since the nation's founding. And so long as the planning is intended to facilitate development, hardly a discouraging word is ever heard. Yet parallel planning for protection of our remaining open space and conservation of our natural resources evokes strident opposition. Land use planning itself, then, is not the issue; rather the question is land use planning for what purpose? Throughout our history, land use planning has been a one-way street down which we relentlessly race toward government-subsidized exploitation of every resource. The question we now face is whether and how to create a parallel process that includes a broader consideration of the public interest in our land and resources.

Our initial attempt to start down this path by creating a biological survey organization did not go well. After hours of fiercely ideological and increasingly partisan debate, it was evident that the arguments for science were not being heard. At the end of the day, we agreed with the bill's sponsors: there was nothing left to do but drag the carcass off and abandon the project. In this first environmental debate of the new Congress, we were hearing a new message: do not expect any help with environmental legislation. The salad days of the 1970s and '80s, when our major environmental laws were enacted with enthusiastic bipartisan support, were over, unlikely to return any time soon.

WHEN THE ENDANGERED SPECIES ACT was enacted in 1973, protecting endangered species was not a controversial idea, even though it was widely understood that the leading cause of extinction was habitat destruction and that habitat destruction was typically a function of uncontrolled human activity—road building, subdivision sprawl, clear-cutting of forests, and inappropriate forms of land use. The sponsors of the legislation acknowledged that to protect endangered species it would be necessary to preserve their habitat, in the words of the act itself, "to provide a means whereby the ecosystems upon which endangered species and threatened species depend may be conserved." And this would require land use planning.

Having diagnosed the problem and stated the need for a remedy, Congress was not very clear in writing the legislation. The act made it a crime to "harass, harm, pursue, hunt, shoot, wound, kill, trap, capture or collect" an endangered species. But what was a landowner to do if her entire ten or one hundred acres was all endangered species habitat? What if she were to cut down a nesting tree to clear a one-acre homesite? Or squashed a listed butterfly?

In 1980, the problem came to a head over a proposed development on San Bruno Mountain, just south of San Francisco, where a developer found that all of his several hundred acres of hillside land was effectively off-limits as the habitat of the endangered mission blue and callippe silverspot butterflies. Congress finally came to the rescue in 1982 when it amended the law. The new provision authorized the U.S. Fish and Wildlife Service to negotiate plans that would give landowners permission to develop land, even though it would mean some incidental destruction of species, provided that enough space were set aside and preserved to give the affected species a fair chance of survival.

By authorizing "habitat conservation plans" Congress invited the agency, and gave it the necessary discretion and latitude, to apply its expertise to work out solutions. Having been thus rescued and effectively encouraged to innovate, however, Fish and Wildlife seemed unwilling to accept or act upon the offer. Cautious, overly deferential to environmentalists opposed to compromise, the agency simply could not seem to get the hang of negotiating habitat conservation plans. Field biologists, trained for tranquil lives out researching the migratory habits of birds and the population dynamics of butterflies, found themselves confronted with rooms packed with angry landowners and hostile environmentalists, each contending that the other had no rights on the land.

Such was the legislative legacy we were faced with in the early 1990s. In 1993, a package of documents came to my office from the Fish and Wildlife Service proposing to list a bird called the California gnatcatcher as an endangered species. The briefing memo was packed with enough biological detail for several graduate theses. The birds nested and foraged on the coastal plain of Southern California, a region classified by biologists as "coastal sage scrub." There were fewer than three thousand mating pairs of gnatcatchers left, far below the ten thousand considered to constitute a viable population for long-term survival. If the gnatcatcher — a small slate gray bird with a call like the meowing of a lost kitten — lacked charisma, it nonetheless was entitled to the same protection as any other species in the ark of creation. The case for action was clear; the necessary documents went to the Federal Register for publication, and the listing took effect several days later.

Then the storm broke. What the briefing memo did not dwell on, and what I had not paid sufficient attention to, was the land use implications. Sage scrub habitat extended across much of the best (and highest priced) undeveloped land remaining between Los Angeles and San Diego. And that meant that, under the law, the land could not be disturbed unless and until such time as we could work out a habitat conservation plan that would permanently dedicate enough coastal sage habitat to guarantee the survival of the species.

By placing the gnatcatcher on the endangered species list, we had, by operation of law, dropped a blanket development moratorium on much of the remaining developable land in the fastest growing real-estate market in California. The California press began reporting on subdivision projects shut down because of the ruling, new projects delayed, banks backing away from construction financing, and construction workers being laid off. Stories circulated of factory workers and retired schoolteachers who had invested their life savings in tracts of land, only to find they were now unable to build on or sell their land because it was the habitat of a bird many had never seen.

The inquiries from White House political staff started flowing in. Was I aware that the president had carried California's fifty-four electoral votes on the way to victory in 1992 and that he would be needing them again for reelection in 1996? Did we really have to put eight hundred square miles of land off-limits for the benefit of a few thousand birds? How long would this go on?

I ruefully conceded that I had not anticipated the political firestorm. Yes, there were only a few thousand birds, but they really did require a lot of space. They did not occupy any one place permanently; they ranged widely across the remaining undeveloped portion of the coastal plain. They needed large connected spaces in which to forage and interbreed and for their population to expand to sufficient size to guarantee survival. It would take time, I explained, to construct a large-scale habitat conservation plan sufficient to protect the bird and thereby allow us to release land for development. The law was clear: until we could come up with a plan, any clearing of land for roads, highways, subdivisions, or any other purpose would be legally risky.

For all the controversy that we were stirring in a sensitive political state, coastal California would eventually prove a good place to work out the conflicts between habitat preservation and development. In the process, we were able to demonstrate how the land use planning implicit in the endangered species legislation could actually be implemented on the ground. Californians seemed ready to accept federal leadership, and the reasons were not hard to discern. The state's coastal regions were home to nearly twenty million people, most of them increasingly agitated by the continual, seemingly unstoppable sprawl that was eroding the very values that had attracted them to California in the first place. On bad days smog blanketed the Los Angeles Basin, freeways were clogged with traffic day and night, and open spaces seemed to recede ever farther into the distance and into memories of the past.

Californians had already begun taking piecemeal steps to control the sprawl through land use planning on their own. In 1972 citizens had voted by initiative to create the California Coastal Commission, vested with strong powers to regulate development along the coastline. Shortly thereafter the state enacted its own Endangered Species Act, modeled on the federal act. Then in 1992, just before we came into office, the state enacted the Natural Communities Conservation Program, a ponderously titled law that would prove important in our efforts to resolve the gnatcatcher controversy. The NCCP granted communities a broad array of new powers to undertake comprehensive programs to preserve open space. The legislation also provided an incentive for landowners to participate; any landowner who voluntarily enrolled an agreed upon portion of his land in open space could be deemed in compliance with the California Endangered Species Act, exempting him from future restrictions on the use of his land.

California is a state in perpetual political flux, spiced by outbursts of populist crusading, endless initiative campaigns, and unpredictable, not to say eccentric, politicians. The NCCP legislation, linking the protection of endangered species with land use planning, was sponsored not by an environmental governor, but by Pete Wilson, a Republican who bore some resemblance to another Californian, Richard Nixon. For Wilson had little real interest in the environment, but like Nixon he rode a wave of public concern to produce some innovative environmental legislation, only to back away from enforcement in the face of controversy.

As with Nixon, Wilson made some excellent environmental appointments, the best of which was his resources secretary, Doug Wheeler, a former president of the Sierra Club. Wheeler had spotted the emerging gnatcatcher problem before we came to office, and, hoping to demonstrate that the NCCP could be made to work on a voluntary basis, he had spent many months traveling up and down the coast, convening meetings of landowners and local officials, explaining the law and encouraging participation. But the effort was going nowhere.

Wheeler and his staff had encountered the realities of open space planning—without a meaningful regulatory sanction, there was little incentive for landowners to participate. Voluntary concessions by an occasional landowner limiting development on her land tended to increase the speculative value accruing to adjacent non-participating landowners who could now, in addition to having a better view over the back fence, anticipate higher land prices because there was less land available for development. It was the recurring governmental dilemma of the "free rider." So long as the rules for protecting open space did not apply to everyone, they were not likely to be embraced by anyone.

Governor Wilson's voluntary program was on the verge of collapse. Unwilling to antagonize the development community, Wilson refused to take the one step necessary to save it: bringing landowners to the table by placing the California gnatcatcher on the state endangered species list, thereby triggering a development moratorium lasting until a habitat protection plan could be worked out.

Then, just as the state program began to fall apart, the federal listing of the gnatcatcher took effect, imposing a development moratorium on much of the coastal plain, the very result the governor had sought to avoid under state law. Suddenly the governor and his state agencies seemed irrelevant as the federal law took hold and placed us in charge of working out a land preservation plan adequate to protect the gnatcatcher from extinction. And, to accomplish that, the biologists were warning us, would require something on the order of several hundred thousand acres of preserves.

We began casting about for a place to begin. Coastal Orange County, bracketed on the south by San Diego and on the north by Los Angeles, seemed the logical place. It still had substantial swaths of open space, and it was less fragmented by development than neighboring counties. Biologists would have more flexibility in designing open space, and we would have a more manageable number of landowners to negotiate with.

We soon discovered, however, that there was just one landowner in Orange County who really mattered: the Irvine Company, holder of a vast Spanish land grant covering a hundred thousand acres and extending from Newport Beach across the coastal plain and into the foothills of the Cleveland National Forest. The Irvine Company was actually just one person, a sole shareholder named Donald Bren. A friend and financial backer of Governor Wilson, Bren was a very private, even reclusive, person who presided over his holdings like a Spanish grandee, attending to every detail, down to the placement of individual palm trees along the medians and open spaces. In conservative Orange County he was accustomed to having things done his way and to public officials who understood who was really in charge. What we were learning did not bode well for a federal wildlife agency about to become a partner in making his land use decisions.

I arranged a discussion with his representatives, agreeing to meet in Phoenix where we would attract less attention than in Washington or in Orange County. The Irvine representatives arrived, accompanied by a member of the Orange County Board of Supervisors, presumably to emphasize that the county would be standing behind any Irvine demands. We began by reviewing the gnatcatcher listing decision. The bird, they explained, really should not be on the endangered species list at all for it was actually just part of a large population of identical gnatcatchers that inhabited Baja California south of the Mexican border. A legal challenge would likely be forthcoming, they argued, since a bird with so many relatives in Mexico could not really be endangered after all. I had heard of Mexico as a safe haven for drug lords, but never for endangered birds.

The Irvine Company, they informed me, had considered joining with building industry groups to file a legal challenge to the gnatcatcher listing. But Donald Bren, they said, did not like to litigate. He had always managed to work out controversies within the county or state, and he would prefer to negotiate with the appropriate federal agencies.

There was room to negotiate, I acknowledged, but any resolution would require a substantial amount of open space dedicated to the preservation of the bird and its habitat. And golf courses would not count. Manicured fairways may be suitable for robins and starlings, but not for gnatcatchers, birds that have evolved over millions of years in close, unbreakable symbiosis with the native plants and insects of the natural sage plains.

Warming to my topic, I explained that even the scattered chunks of native habitat left in patches on hillsides and in ephemeral drainage courses not planned for development probably did not have much biological value. Most native species do not fare well in isolated patches where they do not interbreed easily, are vulnerable to predation, and can easily be wiped out by random events like oil spills or wildfires.

Open space meant different things to developers and to ecologists. To the one it was mostly about enhancing the aesthetic appeal of the landscape for discerning purchasers. To the other it was about taking a bird's-eye view—thinking of how birds attract mates across the landscape, how they select nesting sites, what kind of terrain produces the insects they feed on, and what cover they need in order to fly across the land out of sight of raptors on the prowl for small birds. A legally acceptable plan for their preservation would have to include large expanses of unaltered native vegetation, connected to other protected lands.

The company representatives did not disagree, and I began to sense they knew more about these issues than I was giving them credit for. By the end of our lunch we agreed to instruct our biologists to work together to outline a plan. We also agreed to work to include in the plan not just the gnatcatcher, but all other potentially threatened or endangered species so that we would not need to repeat this process every time another plant or animal appeared on the list.

A big question lurked unanswered, unanswerable without more scientific study: how much land was needed? The biologists had a legal obligation to demand that enough land remain undeveloped to assure survival of the species. And Bren had property rights protected by the Constitution from regulation that went too far in depriving him of reasonable economic use of his land. I wondered whether the two could be reconciled. There were no guidelines; we were entering uncharted regulatory terrain because, in the twenty years since passage of the Endangered Species Act, no planning on this scale had ever been attempted.

As we concluded the meeting, I recalled something I had read about a research park that Bren was developing in partnership with the Irvine campus of the University of California. Bren had donated five hundred acres to the university while reserving another five hundred acres to develop on his own account. The public and the private, in a fifty-fifty split, each added value to the other, perhaps suggesting that development and nature could also be accommodated on a grand and mutually beneficial scale.

As negotiations for an Irvine habitat conservation plan got under way, we turned to San Diego County, California's southernmost county, right on the Mexican border. This area had no hundred-thousand-acre Spanish land grants on which to project and design landscape solutions. In the absence of planning, developments were scattered randomly across the land, climbing up hillsides, perched on mesa tops, and nestled within riverside enclaves, red-tile roofs forming random patterns like brush strokes on an expressionist canvas.

From a look at the maps, it was not obvious where we could even begin. It seemed inconceivable that we could identify and contact each owner of land with remaining sage habitat and then initiate thousands of individual negotiations to cobble together an open space plan. I tried to imagine beleaguered biologists from the Fish and Wildlife Service walking the streets of conservative communities, knocking on doors, announcing they were from the federal government, here to help you work out a habitat conservation plan to save a bird that you have probably never seen. It was enough to make me wish that Donald Bren owned a big chunk of this county as well.

We were stuck in a regulatory cul-de-sac. We had legal authority, yet there was no practical way to use it without the active cooperation of city and county governments willing to use their traditional zoning powers to regulate land use. And there was scant reason to expect local governments to step forward to help us implement a program that was novel and untested, that had never been tried on this scale, at a time when some politicians were inviting their constituents to ignore the law by assuring them it would soon be modified or repealed.

The underlying resistance to land use planning in San Diego, as elsewhere in the country, was not difficult to discern. Local planning and zoning commissions serve landowners with the tacit understanding that rangeland, agricultural land, and other undeveloped open space wherever located, whatever its ecological value, can eventually be rezoned, subdivided, and developed into commercial, residential, or industrial uses when the demand for it appears. The expectation of speculative profit from land ownership is embedded in our culture to the near exclusion of the broader public interest in protecting wildlife, preserving watersheds, and maintaining open space.

The absence of large-scale open space planning in the United States, and the consequent destruction of landscape ecosystems, results from the almost exclusive control of land use decisions by municipal and county governments in thrall to developers and the lure of speculative land profits. The mantra "land use planning is a local matter" denies the reality that we live in a national economy where developers accumulate capital and political power sufficient to overwhelm even well-meaning, part-time local officials and their meager resources. The jurisdiction of local officials ends at the municipal or county boundary; while developers continually threaten to pack up and go across that boundary to the next jurisdiction down the road where local officials will be more pliable and willing to accommodate their demands.

The result of this local culture of accommodation among elected officials, landowners, and developers is that open landscapes, whether habitat for endangered species or just space enough for beauty and wonderment at Creation, continually recede and disappear as development encroaches and consumes them. And even when communities do awaken to the call of open space, zoning bodies are assailed by developers arguing that "just one more exception won't make any difference."

Pondering how to engage with the community in the face of these realities, we circled back to the state government. If we had rescued Governor Wilson's exercise in voluntary land use planning from abject failure, we in turn were teetering on the brink of our own failure. It was becoming excruciatingly clear that neither of us could make this work without the other. Though we had provided California with the missing ingredient of a development moratorium, only California could provide us with the necessary credibility, capacity for outreach to local communities, and planning capabilities. It was time to reach across partisan lines and try for a working partnership with the state.

WITH THE DEVELOPMENT moratorium imposed by the Endangered Species Act, we had provided state officials the means to make their Natural Communities Conservation Program work. With minor exceptions, lands would be released for development only upon completion of open space plans that were acceptable to the state and that also met the requirements of the federal law. As the state's resource secretary, Doug Wheeler now became my equal partner in the process of constructing an effective system of preserves in San Diego County.

Over the next year our staffs worked with San Diego city and county planners, producing mountains of topographic maps, habitat surveys, land tenure records, economic studies, and species inventories, all the while attending hundreds of public meetings to hear citizen responses. Previously reticent local officials stepped forward, more eager to work with their state officials than just with federal agencies.

With no dominant landowner to work with and a landscape badly fragmented by development, the preserve plans for San Diego County emerged more slowly and painfully than anything we had encountered in Orange County. The preserves would have to be stitched together from thousands of landholdings through careful use of zoning incentives to protect sufficient area while freeing less critical land for development. On smaller tracts and as a condition of developing them, landowners could opt to purchase other land designated for protection as mitigation. And in some areas outright purchases by the county would prove to be the appropriate solution.

As the plans progressed, that ultimate arbiter of political direction, public opinion, began moving our way. The San Diego Zoo, a premier charity of the San Diego establishment, with a strong program directed toward conserving endangered species, began a campaign to gain community acceptance. Members of Congress, Republicans and Democrats, sensing public support, began to bring home modest federal grants to help the process along.

Back in Orange County the Irvine Company made ready to announce the completion of its central Orange County habitat conservation plan, establishing two permanent preserves that totaled more than thirty thousand acres to provide habitat protection for the gnatcatcher and thirty-two other species of concern. We gathered for the dedication ceremony on a hillside meadow bordered by groves of oak and sycamore.

As we pushed through the tall grass up the hill to the ceremony's site on Irvine Ranch, I turned to Doug Wheeler and exclaimed, "How did this happen? We are approaching a presidential election year. Your governor is preparing to run against my president. The Endangered Species Act stirs controversy. Yet we have completed an unprecedented open space plan without having sparked a divisive political fight over property rights. And now here we are, together with the largest developer in California, all eager to take a share of the credit."

He reflected a moment and replied, "Public support. And good press. The fact that we worked together. The press could explain what we were trying to do, rather than covering another political quarrel. And Donald Bren. You know that he's a friend and big supporter of the governor, and I expect that had a lot to do with it."

The settlement at Irvine Ranch was a defining moment in the emergence of the Endangered Species Act as a land use planning statute, capable of forging a balance between development and the preservation of large ecosystems. Fortunately, Bren was out to solve a problem and in the process he had given credibility to a statute that might not have survived much longer without some demonstrable evidence that it could be made to work on private property.

Then in 1998, the City of San Diego and San Diego County approved large-scale habitat plans. The plans took in nearly two hundred thousand acres of crucial sage habitats, stream corridors, and vernal pools throughout the county, protecting essential habitat for more than one hundred species, including the least Bell's vireo, the whip-tailed lizard, a number of invertebrates, a long list of plants endemic to the region, and of course the gnatcatcher. These plans demonstrated that the Endangered Species Act could be made to work even on complex, partially developed landscapes with highly fragmented ownership.

YET, FOR ALL THE SUCCESS, the San Diego plan was hardly perfect, either in coping with evolving patterns of urban development or for preserving the endangered species and biological diversity of the coastal plain ecosystem. The landscape planning, driven by the Endangered Species Act, came mostly after the highways and subdivision tracts had already fragmented much of the landscape. Rather than cobbling together remaining patches of open space after the fact, planning of land use patterns — for both development and for preservation of the natural world — clearly should take place earlier, as in Orange County, while there is still time and space enough to design an appropriate separation of town and country, setting cities in a matrix of open landscapes that retain more of their ecological functions.

Ideally, cities on the land should be visualized like an archipelago, as islands surrounded by a sea of open landscapes. Like islands, cities should be compact, self-sustaining, with discernable outer boundaries, beyond which the landscapes are devoted to agriculture and the preservation of space and biological diversity. How many islands, how large each island should be, and the patterns of development within each island are questions best left for local decision, shaped by variable patterns of demographics, culture, climate, economics, and just plain random chance. The overarching national interest, properly the subject of federal legislation, is in the surrounding natural landscapes that sustain our rivers and lakes, support wildlife and fisheries, and that comprise the ecosystems that provide for us and the diversity of life on our planet.

The concept of city limits as something more than a jurisdictional line on a map, as the place where the city actually ends and the country begins, is an ancient concept. The cities of antiquity were surrounded by walls built and maintained to keep out enemy armies. Thucydides has left us a memorable description of the walls surrounding Athens and the adjoining port of Piraeus, which anchored the Athenian defensive strategy against the invading Spartans in the Peloponnesian War. Time and time again, the Spartans invaded, only to fall short as the Athenians withdrew into their walled city. In the end, however, the Athenians succumbed, as the Spartans waged a war of attrition, returning repeatedly to destroy the wheat fields, olive orchards, and vineyards that lay outside the walls.

In the Middle Ages, with the invention of gunpowder and cannon, offensive warfare gained ascendancy and urban boundaries established by defensive walls became obsolete, remaining only to be admired and photographed by future tourists and students. Until the twentieth century, though, outward urban expansion was limited by the time constraints of travel; you could only commute so far to work by horseback or carriage. In our time the automobile and the urban freeway have largely erased that constraint, and cities have expanded outward virtually without limit.

In the years following World War II a regional planning movement gained momentum, premised on the idea that in the emerging metropolitan areas growth could be managed only by new agencies with the power to coordinate planning—including transportation infrastructure and water and sewer systems—across local political boundaries. Washington, the nation's first planned city thanks to George Washington and Pierre L'Enfant, was the natural center of these efforts. In 1962, the National Capital Planning Commission published alternate planning models to guide the urban expansion of Washington and the surrounding areas of Maryland and Virginia, including one for construction of several designed "dispersed cities," which would be new towns located ten

to thirty miles outside the existing metropolitan area with intervening areas to be preserved as open space. Another model, the "radial
corridor," in which development would radiate outward in spokes
with the wedges in between the spokes as open space, was the final
choice of the planners. It was widely publicized and praised by
many, including President Kennedy.

As is evident to any visitor, the various plans eventually fell by the
wayside, ignored by political decision makers. The metropolitan
area has continued its pell-mell outward expansion toward the
Piedmont, along Chesapeake Bay, up the Shenandoah Valley and
northward toward Pennsylvania, leading to acrimonious fights
over more roads and freeways and leaving only the L'Enfant core
city as a reminder of a distant time when city planning had a larger,
or at least more effective, constituency. Since that time regional
planning around the country has largely meant facilitating development and sprawl by coordinating development of roads and infrastructure.

In 1969 a disastrous oil spill in the Santa Barbara channel
brought an outpouring of concern over coastal degradation that
prompted the Congress to enact the Coastal Zone Management
Act of 1972. The CZMA, as it came to be known, set up a true
federal-state land use planning structure for the coastal regions of
the country. Designed for the protection of coastal environments, it
marked an important shift toward land use planning for the primary purpose, not of urban design, but of protecting open spaces—
in this case coastal waters, tributaries, and shorelines—as an ecological imperative.

In that same year the Nixon administration joined with Senator
Henry Jackson to introduce the Land Use Policy and Planning
Assistance Act, which proposed grants to encourage the states to
identify and regulate areas of special concern, including large-scale
developments and "areas of critical environmental concern." The
resulting state plans would be subject to federal review. And states

that did not participate would be subject to withholding of up to 21 percent of their share of federal highway and airport development funds.

The bill, amended on the floor to eliminate the withholding sanction, passed the Senate in 1972 and again in 1973. Then in 1974 a companion House bill went down to defeat after President Nixon, reversing position, withdrew his support. This failed effort marked the high tide of federal land use initiatives, and in the thirty some years since then the Congress has not returned to the subject.

At about the same time at the state level in Oregon, Governor Tom McCall had in his first term proposed and pushed through the legislature popular measures to protect the state's beaches and coastlines. Then, in his second term, he expanded his vision to propose a statewide land use plan. Encountering strong opposition from real-estate developers, utilities, and the forest industry, McCall created a crisis by using his emergency powers to impose a development moratorium on several coastal communities where uncontrolled sewer discharges from new subdivisions were fouling nearby beaches.

In response the Oregon legislature enacted a comprehensive land use law that included formation of a state commission empowered to write strong regulations, a process that eventually produced the urban growth boundary regulations for which Oregon is known. In essence the law drew a circle around the outskirts of existing communities and stipulated that the undeveloped land outside the circle had to remain in nonurban uses such as agriculture and forestry. The growth boundaries included a unique feature designed to prevent them from strangling cities and towns: once established, the boundaries were not permanently fixed, but were elastic, subject to outward adjustment so as to maintain sufficient land inventory on the city periphery to continually accommodate twenty years of projected growth. This measure of flexibility was an innovation in response to lessons learned from London and other

European cities where urban boundaries fixed in place by designated greenbelts often failed as growth leapt over the greenbelts to continue outward.

In its thirty-year existence the Oregon law has had a dramatic effect on the state's landscape, especially in the Willamette Valley, where farms, forests, and vineyards still cover unbroken rural landscapes adjacent to Portland, Eugene, and other cities, in welcome contrast to the sprawling communities that are destroying the remaining rivers and farmlands of inland California and southern Arizona.

Critics have characterized Oregon's law as controlled sprawl, rather than true planning, for it does allow outward expansion and it says nothing about the urban form within the boundary, a topic left for traditional local planning and zoning procedures. Nonetheless, for thirty years the law commanded the support of a majority of Oregonians, who voted down several ballot initiatives to weaken its provisions. Until 2004, that is, when property-rights advocates sponsored a ballot initiative requiring the state to compensate current landowners for any diminution in value of their land caused by a land use regulation imposed while they owned the land. While the impact of this initiative on the Oregon land use plan will probably not be clear for years to come, it serves as a reminder that open space plans must be designed and implemented with careful attention to the perception and reality of landowner economic expectations for use of their property.

Even as the Oregon experience continues to unfold, other communities have taken different approaches to open space. And, as in southern California, the Endangered Species Act has provided the catalyst to many of these efforts.

LAS VEGAS AT FIRST glance looks like the last place you would find a fresh, contemporary approach to creating urban boundaries of any sort, much less using a law such as the Endangered Species Act. The city revels in its reputation for rampant, unrestrained growth. Its population has doubled to more than a million and a half residents in the last decade. Water shortages? Well, yes, but the city responds by offering residents a dollar a square foot to tear up lawns and replace them with cactus so that enough water can be saved to allow builders to create still more subdivisions. State land use regulations? Not much there beyond regulating casinos and bordellos.

Driving across Las Vegas by daylight past new freeway excavations, subdivision for-sale signs, and rows of newly framed housing starts provides few clues to the existence of anything resembling an urban boundary. The best way to see what is happening is to go into downtown Las Vegas, to a casino called the Stratosphere Tower, and to ride the elevator to the observation deck just before sunset. At first there is not much to see in the glaring afternoon light, but as the sun sets behind the Spring Mountains and the sky darkens, the patterns begin to emerge. The city is an island of bright lights, with shorelines where the city stops and beyond that nothing, no lights at all, just darkness, like looking out to sea from the land. The nighttime city is an island of light in a desert archipelago.

The search for an explanation takes us back into history, which for Las Vegas is a relatively short period commencing a half century ago. Before World War II Las Vegas was a small crossroads town, surrounded by barren desert—land so dry and uninviting that most of it remained in federal ownership for lack of homesteaders willing to gamble on survival. After the war entrepreneurs and mobsters arrived to create a gambling oasis, and modern Las Vegas soon emerged. As the city continued to expand, developers began clamoring for the federal government to open up the public lands surrounding the city for development.

Then as the city grew, a legendary California congressman named Phil Burton entered the picture. His San Francisco constituents cared little about southern Nevada, but they were concerned about Lake Tahoe, where a boom in shoreline hotel and condominium development was threatening the lake, world-renowned for the purity and emerald clarity of its waters. In 1980

Burton joined with Nevada congressman Jim Santini to put forth a novel proposal—to slow growth at Lake Tahoe by promoting growth in Las Vegas. The key to preserving Lake Tahoe was obtaining money to purchase expensive shoreline lands. And the key to obtaining the money lay in selling federal lands surrounding Las Vegas for development.

Since Lake Tahoe straddles the California-Nevada state line, Burton had little difficulty persuading the Nevada congressional delegation to support the idea. Then, to assuage congressional skeptics fearful of diverting an endless flow of Nevada land-sale receipts away from the federal treasury, Burton and Santini agreed to limit land sales to no more than seven hundred acres each year from the immediate vicinity of Las Vegas.

Federal land managers then implemented the law by drawing a large square centered on Las Vegas, approximately ten miles on a side, within which lands would be selected for sale. This Burton-Santini square, as it came to be known, created not to plan Las Vegas but to preserve Lake Tahoe, became, for a time at least, a de facto urban boundary around Las Vegas.

Subsequently, however, as Las Vegas continued to expand outward, developers began agitating to breach the Burton-Santini square. And, for all its symbolic significance, there was nothing in law that specifically prohibited the Bureau of Land Management from disposing of desert lands outside the boundary. Just as another unconstrained land rush seemed about to begin, two new actors appeared—the ancient, slow-moving desert tortoise and a new, energetic U.S. senator named Harry Reid.

Reid began his career as a pro-growth senator who was also interested in establishing protected areas out back of beyond. In short order he compiled an impressive record that included legislation creating Great Basin National Park and expanding the Stillwater National Wildlife Refuge. Then he began to see opportunities in southern Nevada where most of the state's population lived. The

Las Vegas valley, he realized, was surrounded on four sides by mountains that would make a natural expansion boundary for the city.

Thinking of the surrounding landscape from an urban perspective, Reid began to advocate that Las Vegas, on its way to becoming a great city, needed outdoor space for parks and recreation and wildlife preservation. Las Vegas needed open space, he said, not to limit growth, but to make it even more attractive for growth.

He began by looking west toward the colored cliffs and canyons at the base of the Spring Mountains, an area resembling the well-known red-rock vistas of northern Arizona and southern Utah. In 1990 Reid persuaded Congress to enclose two hundred thousand acres within a newly created Red Rock Canyon National Conservation Area.

Encouraged by the positive public response, Reid next looked south. The area was still several miles beyond the development fringe, there was still plenty of close-in land to build on, and the mountain slopes were not yet in demand. In 2002 he obtained legislation designating nearly fifty thousand acres in the McCullough Range as the federally protected Sloan Canyon National Conservation Area. To the north of Las Vegas, the mountains were already protected as part of the Desert National Wildlife Refuge, created in 1936 to protect the desert bighorn sheep. That left only the French Mountains on the eastern margins of the city unprotected.

Much of Reid's circle of protected mountain lands had thus taken shape. What it lacked, however, was a connective matrix of lower-elevation lands to bind the mountain heights into a unified whole. If these remaining gaps of low desert that surrounded the mountains were not protected, political pressures for outward expansion seemed destined to burst the gossamer map lines of the Burton-Santini square and eventually reach up the sloping gravel fans and through the gaps, isolating the mountain fronts in a surrounding mass of development.

It was the Endangered Species Act, as applied to the circumstances of the threatened desert tortoise, that supplied the glue to fit all the mountain pieces together in a consolidated urban boundary. The desert tortoise, an animal with an intricate, engraved carapace resembling a Toledo inlay design, had survived and prospered for eons on this land—until ranchers arrived with their huge herds of cattle and sheep. After a century of competition from grazing livestock and habitat destruction from road building and development, the tortoise had made its way onto the endangered species list.

When the tortoise was listed, its habitat became off-limits to development. The habitat favored by the tortoise consists of the sandy, gently sloping alluvial fans extending outward from the mountains, which is a good description of the areas most coveted by developers. And as in Southern California, it was the development moratorium that galvanized city leaders, who feared a slowdown in the home-building industry, to cooperate in working out a habitat protection plan. The basic planning principle was simple: expand the Burton-Santini boundary to a final, permanent perimeter, designating the lands outside the revised boundary as tortoise reserves.

To complete the reserves it remained only to purchase a few scattered private tracts, mostly old homesteads in the outlying areas, and to retire the grazing rights that went with them. To fund the purchases, developers agreed to pay a mitigation fee of $565 for each new subdivision lot developed. Las Vegas home builders, accustomed to paying development fees to finance infrastructure such as roads, sewers, schools, and neighborhood parks, did not object to paying another fee, so long as they could put the check in the mail and get on with leveling the land for construction.

In 1999 Senator Reid invited me to the dedication ceremony for the multiple-species habitat conservation plan. The plan established protected desert tortoise reserves that would surround much of the city, filling in the spaces between the mountain parks and wilderness areas. After the biologists explained the significance of the unique plant and animal assemblages of the surrounding Mojave Desert, Reid spoke. These reserves, he explained would be good for growth, they would make Las Vegas a more attractive place for families, providing recreational value easily accessible for Sunday afternoon outings. He never once mentioned the words "urban boundary" or "land use planning" or "growth limitation." His remarks could have been written by the chamber of commerce or the home builders' association.

The emerging urban boundary in Las Vegas is not complete; development is still leaking outward in a corridor toward Henderson and Lake Mead to the southeast and through a gap toward the northwest. And the Las Vegas experience is undeniably unique to its time and place. Nonetheless, looking beyond the place-specific details, there are three important lessons that can be drawn from these events.

Lesson one is the manner in which Reid managed to separate the issues of growth and protection of open space in the minds of his constituents. Voters know him as a growth advocate, second to none in his promotion of new industry, job creation, expanding the Las Vegas water supply, and obtaining federal funds for highways, mass transit, and a new regional airport thirty miles south of the city. So long as his open space proposals were not perceived as threatening the ongoing real-estate boom, he remained free to take steps whose true implications lay in the future, not in this generation but for those yet to come.

Lesson two: Reid began with a good feel for the surrounding landscape, aware that mountain heights have inherent appeal as places that should be preserved for the view from city neighborhoods and for public access. He started with the best known and most scenic locale and then built on that success by gradually extending his efforts to other parts of the surrounding valley heights.

The third general lesson from Las Vegas is that urban boundaries should be designed to fit loosely, allowing cities to grow up to them, providing time and space for adjustments to take place, including infill and more compact development.

Las Vegas for the most part now has in place a workable urban growth boundary, assuring a clean division between human and natural space. This urban island, viewed from the Stratosphere Tower, will likely be seen to expand in concentric rings for another decade. But it will then reach the preset boundaries of an island in a wilderness archipelago.

TUCSON IS A CITY that I knew well from my days as governor of Arizona. Tucson has always been sensitive to its surroundings, a place deeply rooted in the Sonoran Desert with its sahuaro forests, springtime displays of flowering trees and plants, and dramatic mountain vistas. The quest for a balance between human habitat and preservation of the natural world has engaged generations of residents, including writers Joseph Wood Krutch, Edward Abbey, Charles Bowden, and Lawrence Clark Powell; political leaders like the Udall brothers, Stewart and Morris; and legions of citizen activists.

For more than a generation, though, Tucson had repeatedly tried and failed to assert control over outward sprawl into the surrounding desert. Until recently this history has mainly offered lessons about how not to approach the interrelated issues of urban planning and open space.

Tucson first attempted to manage growth by limiting the supply of water. The platform for this effort was the Central Arizona Project, a federal reclamation project authorized in 1968 to build a three-hundred-mile aqueduct to bring Colorado River water to Phoenix and Tucson.

At the outset nearly everyone supported the CAP. Then in the mid-1970s, as the canal then under construction approached Tucson, environmentalists began having second thoughts, questioning whether the city really needed to grow on the scale of Los Angeles. Tucson, they concluded, could do just fine with existing groundwater supplies, eventually building out as a medium-sized, sustainable desert city determined not to emulate the spiraling growth, congestion, and declining quality of life already becoming apparent in Phoenix. By choosing to forgo imported water supplies, Tucson would in effect be imposing a cap, however indeterminate the exact number might be, on future population growth.

In 1974 Tucson residents elected a new city council dominated by growth skeptics who soon proposed a series of water-conservation measures, intended at least in part to demonstrate that properly managed groundwater supplies would be sufficient for the future of the city. The development community, however, saw the proposals as a plot to undermine the case for bringing in new water supplies. In the ensuing controversy, several council members were recalled and replaced by traditional CAP supporters. The anti-growth movement seemed to fade, and by 1990 the aqueduct project, with its cornucopia of imported water promising a seemingly unlimited future, reached Tucson.

What the Tucson managed-growth advocates had learned from the CAP fight was that proposals to shape growth by limiting water supplies are a hard, if not impossible sell. Water in the west, and for that matter most everywhere else, is an iconic resource never to be passed up. No city, with the possible exception of an occasional upscale enclave like Santa Barbara or Marin County, is ever likely to cap growth by foregoing water that will only be claimed by someone else. Tucson was not about to see its share of the Colorado River go unused, only to be taken up by Phoenix and other communities elsewhere in the state.

To be sure, some communities will face water limits imposed by environmental considerations such as the need to protect lakes and rivers, but that argument was not available in Tucson. And in some cases cities can use water effectively to direct growth by the simple expedient of refusing to extend water service to proposed developments.

With completion of the CAP, the city's water supplies assured, the population of greater Tucson continued to explode, doubling from three hundred thousand to six hundred thousand and again to nearly a million, a growth rate that reignited the debate over sprawl and destruction of the surrounding Sonoran Desert. And with increasing growth throughout the state, uncontrolled sprawl once again became a hot political issue. In 2001 polls showed that 70 percent of Arizonans would favor measures to control growth, and the Sierra Club launched a statewide ballot initiative, loosely modeled on the Oregon law, that would require Arizona cities to establish urban growth boundaries.

Once again developers and home builders rushed forward to stigmatize the initiative as a no-growth measure, designed to limit population growth and economic expansion. Proponents were slow to explain that containing sprawl was not equivalent to restricting growth, that the two phenomena were entirely distinct and that establishment of urban boundaries could exemplify what has come to be called "smart growth," focusing on infill and some increased density within the footprint of existing urban space. But few voters considered the Sierra Club to be a reliable guide in the ongoing quest for balance and sustainability. The proposal, complex and difficult to explain, went down by a resounding 70 to 30 margin.

Uncomprehending as a mule being whacked with a two-by-four, those on the environmental side seemed unable to absorb the lesson: open space proposals that can be stigmatized as limiting growth are not likely to succeed. The score in Tucson was growth advocates two, environmentalists zero.

In the meantime, as the growth-boundary argument waxed and waned, Tucson conservationists got a third chance. An open space movement began on public land, was furthered by the Endangered Species Act, and grew into a comprehensive county open space plan extending considerably beyond the requirements of the act.

In 1999 I met with the Pima County Board of Supervisors to discuss how the Department of the Interior could assist efforts to preserve open space and to implement a growth-management plan within the county. Examining the maps, we noted that more than half the land in the Las Cienegas Valley on the southeast margin of Tucson was still in federal ownership, administered by the Bureau of Land Management. We organized a field trip to Las Cienegas, accompanied by environmentalists, landowners, and members of the press.

Las Cienegas, Spanish for "desert wetlands," is an oak savanna cradled between two high mountain ranges, the Whetstones on the east and the Santa Ritas on the west. Once the headquarters of the Empire Ranch, the valley is traversed by a small perennial stream coursing through thickets of willow and sedges, shaded by cottonwoods and sycamores. The expanding suburbs of Tucson were advancing toward the valley, a few scattered tracts already had been split up into subdivisions, and it did not require much imagination to see what the future held.

After traveling the length of the valley we gathered at the adobe ranch house, once the Empire Ranch headquarters, for lunch on the patio, after which we spread out the maps and talked. We began, as with most land discussions, with excursions into history, prompted by examining the land tenure patterns shown in various colors on the maps. The valley was still primarily public land, but heavily intermixed with private holdings, a pattern evolved through generations of homesteading and mining claims. The land had been ruled by many sovereigns — first the Apaches, then Spain, followed by Mexico, then it became part of the Territory of New Mexico, then the Arizona Territory, and finally statehood. Title to the land, it seemed, was constantly changing, but the land itself did not seem to change much; it had been ranchland for four centuries and Indian hunting grounds before that. Now, in an instant of time this stream of history was about to be submerged beneath acres of asphalt and concrete.

The county supervisors, responsive to environmental sentiment in Tucson, leaned toward designating the valley as conservation lands. Most of the ranchers disagreed. It was their right, and nobody else's, they said, to decide. Small landowners and local homeowners were divided, some wishing to protect their rural lifestyle, others eager to profit from an increase in land values that development would bring.

As the afternoon wore on and the shadows cast by the summits of the Santa Ritas began enveloping the valley, it was clear there would not be much consensus, no matter how long we talked. As long as ranchers and the large landowners had nothing to lose, why should they negotiate? And absent agreement on some form of protection, elected officials were not likely to act and the status quo would prevail. In the Las Cienegas Valley in Arizona, as throughout most of the nation, the presumption still persists — embedded in local politics and economics — that development should occur and that the course of that development should be left to individual landowners acting to maximize their own land values, selling out to developers at the most opportune moment. If consensus meant that landowners must agree, and if consensus was the condition for conservation, then the valley was doomed to fall into the spreading suburbanization of Tucson, its value as open space gone forever. We had reached an impasse, a standoff familiar to every local official and every conservationist in the nation.

Finally I made a suggestion: since we could not reach agreement perhaps I could return to Washington and recommend to President Clinton that he issue an executive order under the Antiquities Act designating the valley as a national monument, a power available to the president wherever there are sizeable blocks of federal land that have not been previously designated for special uses. By putting that proposal on the table, I established a default position; in the absence of consensus the land would be permanently protected, thereby reversing the normal presumption that in the absence of consensus development goes forward.

The shadows seemed to deepen as groups of participants caucused among themselves. Now there were real incentives to find a workable alternative more to their liking than a unilateral federal land designation. The balance of power had suddenly shifted — from landowners with the power to perpetuate the status quo simply by refusing to agree, to a president with the power to upend that status quo by invoking a national law to assert the public interest in the future of the valley.

Finally someone asked the relevant question: would I be willing to defer a monument recommendation to give the parties time to meet with their congressional representatives and work out a piece of legislation? They needed time to discuss issues such as boundaries of a conservation area and whether grazing should be continued as a permitted use. I agreed. Legislation would be a more lasting and acceptable solution precisely because it would afford all participants the opportunity to be heard through their elected representatives. I reminded those gathered that they would have to act quickly, and that I would recommend that the president veto any bill that did not provide meaningful protection for this valley.

The following year Congress enacted legislation to establish the Las Cienegas National Conservation Area, something of a record for a relatively intricate piece of land conservation legislation. Republicans, by then in control of Congress, had taken the lead at the request of the landowners acting through their congressman, Jim Kolbe. Democrats, empowered by the possibility of a presidential veto, had participated to their satisfaction, yielding a result both tailored to the needs of the local community and consistent with the larger national goal of protecting open space and the environment.

WHILE LAS CIENEGAS PROVIDED an important piece of open space on one margin of Tucson, it was hardly a comprehensive open space plan. It was the Endangered Species Act that would again provide the framework, as it had in California and Las Vegas, to crystallize community support for a more comprehensive plan. Another bird provided the impetus—the cactus ferruginous pygmy-owl that nests in the trees and sahuaro forests of the Sonoran Desert. After biologists found only seventy-four of the birds in all of southern Arizona, the bird was listed as endangered in 1998. Most of the developing areas of Tucson lay within owl habitat, so once again the red light was flashing, confronting developers with a moratorium on subdividing in those areas of the county that constituted owl habitat.

The initial reaction to the listing in Tucson played according to script. The usual suspects—developers, the chamber of commerce, home-builder and property-rights advocates—appeared on cue to call for repeal of the Endangered Species Act. At first the prospects for a cooperative federal-state solution did not appear good. In Arizona there was no Donald Bren among the developers, and no Harry Reid in the state's congressional delegation. And in Phoenix, with a governor continually voicing opposition to the Endangered Species Act, there was no Doug Wheeler to engage state agencies in crafting solutions.

All that remained was the Pima County Board of Supervisors, consisting of five elected officials who happened to be well aware of the divisive fights of the past, keenly attuned to their environmentally oriented electorates, and ready to build upon the opportunity presented by the owl moratorium. What followed was two years of meetings, hearings, and draft plans and revisions, all of which highlighted the need for protecting large blocks of habitat. County officials had by then observed and assimilated the experiences of Orange County and San Diego County, and they made a momentous decision—to take the process to the next level by preparing a comprehensive land use and open space plan for the county, encompassing not just the habitat of the owl and other threatened species, but drawn with the objective of protecting riparian areas, outlying rangeland, and other important ecosystems throughout the county. What finally emerged was a general land use plan, dedicating extensive areas of undeveloped land to open space through an adroit combination of public acquisition and regulation. Pima County had accomplished a first—using the listing moratorium as a springboard from which to develop, not just the legally required habitat conservation plan, but an entirely new open space plan.

In 2003 the board of supervisors formally adopted the Sonoran Desert Conservation Plan and set in motion the zoning changes and land acquisition proposals for implementation. In the spring of 2004 voters approved a $130 million dollar bond measure to begin land acquisition. Tucson had finally, after thirty years of starts and stops, found the appropriate formula for open space preservation, something that had eluded it in the earlier fights over water allocation and mandated growth boundaries.

TUCSON WAS NOT ALONE in seeking a bond issue to finance land acquisition for open space. In that same 2004 election cycle, voters in thirty states approved more than three billion dollars in such bond issues. There is also evidence that landowners are beginning to awaken to the need for conservation and to invest personally in land preservation. A striking example is occurring in the Red Hills of southern Georgia and northern Florida that border on the rapidly expanding urban area of Tallahassee. There, owners of the quail hunting plantations on the northern fringe of the city have begun donating conservation easements totalling some 130,000 acres, more than a third of land in the Red Hills region.

Private efforts, however, are not in themselves sufficient to protect large landscapes. What remains lacking are large-scale plans to maximize the value of open space. Such plans require government leadership and the willingness to use all the tools, public and private, available for land protection. What is needed is a larger vision for the patterns on the land that we want to see in place a century from now.

If, as I believe, the Endangered Species Act has been the key to success in the three urban areas discussed at length in this chapter, why have these results not been more widely replicated in other parts of the country, especially in the Northeast where expanding urban and suburban areas have remained largely outside the provisions of the act? The principal reason is that in these regions there are relatively few endangered species with broad habitat requirements, such as birds, which have typically driven application of the Endangered Species Act. By whatever accidents of climate, landscape diversity, and patterns of human development, endangered species tend to be concentrated in the southern and western parts of the country, leaving other regions less subject to provisions of the act.

Supporters and critics alike have cited as a weakness the eleventh hour, after-the-fact structure of the act, which dictates that species receive protection only when they have declined to the brink of extinction. As a remedy, the statute should be expanded to apply before the fact of endangerment, more in the style of preventive medicine, designed to assure the health of the patient before debilitating illness sets in.

The Endangered Species Act has not been significantly amended since 1982 and by any calculation it is past time to revise and update it. The amendments proposed to date by both proponents and opponents of the act have been relatively narrow, focusing on technical changes in the science of listing, in determining the extent of habitat that should receive legal protection, and in strengthening the role of the states in administrating the act—all significant issues that merit attention.

But technical amendments, however necessary, are not sufficient. The act should be amended to build upon the success stories, not just in identifying and listing species, but in transforming habitat requirements into effective land use plans. It should contain a broad mandate to identify and protect landscapes and watersheds and critical ecosystems, whether or not an endangered species happens to be in the neighborhood at a particular time. It should be expanded to include not just endangered species, but to promote the protection of open space and important watersheds, forests, and other threatened ecosystems—before the downward spiral to extinction begins. We should begin to think of the Endangered Species Act, not in bits and pieces, but as an effective mandate to conserve the ecosystems upon which all of life, including human life, depends.

An improved Endangered Species Act, revised to include proactive protection of open space and critical ecosystems, would properly require a larger role for the states and their local governments, including cities and especially counties. The Southern California experience provides rich instructive material for how such a federal-state system could be constructed. And, as previously noted, an existing federal law, the Coastal Zone Management Act, offers yet another suggestive model for a broader federal-state effort to protect ecosystems and open space.

The CZMA offers grants and technical assistance to coastal states willing to adopt coastal zone land use plans that meet federal standards. It also offers another inducement, giving participating states a qualified right of veto over the issuance of federal permits for coastal activities such as location of port facilities, offshore drilling, and other developments. Since the program's inception, thirty-four of thirty-five eligible states have signed on. The key to this program's success is the way in which it trades a federal role in preparation of land use plans for a state role in federal permitting activities, a nice formulation of participatory federalism.

A comprehensive federal-state ecosystem and open space planning approach, whether in the form of an expanded Endangered Species Act or a separate statute, would begin with statutory standards. Defining standards for open space is admittedly a more complex task than setting numerical limits for air quality or water pollution, which is not to suggest that it can't be done. Already efforts are under way in several states that point the way toward success. In Massachusetts, Arizona, and other states, The Nature Conservancy has begun to publish maps of "heritage landscapes," selected based on multiple criteria such as the presence of rare and endemic species, unique geology, and protection of significant streams and watersheds. In California, the state's biodiversity council is compiling statewide maps of priority open space to be protected for biological and scenic and historical values. And as previously noted, the emerging land use plan for Pima County establishes a system of open space protection based on the mapping of core biological protection areas within the county. Still lacking in almost all states, however, is an overall vision that would lead to enforceable laws for conferring protection upon selected landscapes.

An effective federal-state open space program must have incentives for states and local governments to participate. The time-honored method of involving states in cooperative programs is through federal grants to states willing to meet the standards set out in federal legislation. In this case, states might qualify by adopting open space programs that meet federal standards and that employ an appropriate range of tools, including zoning, density transfers, land exchanges, mitigation credits, protective agricultural zoning, proper planning of highway and infrastructure programs, and purchases or donations of land or conservation easements to create significant protected landscapes.

Successful federal-state programs typically include sanctions, as well as incentives, to encourage state participation. The Clean Air Act provides an instructive example. It sets national air quality goals and standards (with attainment failures regularly reported in the press). It then delegates administrative responsibility to the states, requiring them to prepare what are known as State Implementation Plans to control sources of air pollution.

The Clean Air Act also authorizes the Environmental Protection Agency to withhold federal highway funds from any state or city that fails to adopt and enforce an effective program. The prospect of losing highway funds is, to paraphrase Samuel Johnson, like the prospect of a hanging—it serves to concentrate the mind. If air-quality programs are not popular, highway construction programs assuredly are. And the two are logically related: building more highways induces more traffic, which causes still more air pollution. And why spend more money to further pollute the skies in states and cities that refuse to take meaningful steps to reduce air pollution?

The same technique might be used in a national open space program, and for essentially the same reason—the leading cause of the destruction of natural landscapes is scattered development brought on and facilitated by freeways and highways, many built or subsidized by federal grants. If states are to have federal highway grants, such monies should at least be conditioned upon meaningful and comprehensive open space programs.

Is it realistic, one may ask, to suggest expanding land protection programs in a season when the Bush administration and Congress are intent not upon expanding, but upon shrinking the reach of our environmental laws? Perhaps progress will not come easily, or at all, in the short run. History, however, instructs us that the trajectory of environmental protection is moving ever upward over time, even as the trend line occasionally breaks downward. And that suggests to me that the seeds of change must be planted now, even if they do not germinate immediately. A familiar anecdote from President Kennedy makes the point: "The great French Marshal Lyautey . . . once asked his gardener to plant a tree. The gardener objected that the tree was slow-growing and would not reach maturity for a hundred years. The Marshal replied, 'In that case, there is no time to lose, plant it this afternoon.'"

What's the Matter with Iowa?

IN THE SUMMER OF 1986 my wife Hattie and I took a bike ride across Iowa along with six thousand others in an annual event sponsored by the *Des Moines Register*. At the end of each day we descended upon another small and picturesque town, put up our tents in parks and along the roads, and swarmed through the town square, mingling with musicians and searching out food vendors. It was a memorable week; we were strangers telling our stories and bonding in the fellowship of the open road, reminiscent of scenes from Chaucer's *Canterbury Tales*. We were riding bikes, not horses, but our destination was also a place of some spiritual significance, the waters of the Mississippi River.

If the towns were picturesque and the residents gracious and friendly, I gradually came to a different impression about the landscapes through which we traveled. At first, as we started off in the milky morning light from Council Bluffs above the Missouri River, the land seemed fresh and exotic, almost tropical in its green profusion.

For hours, we pedaled along roads bordered by fields of tall corn, still shooting upward, powered by the intense summer sun. The landscape hardly varied; the cornfields passed by unbroken except for alternating fields of soybeans. By the second day and the third, it grew monotonous, like staring at the sea from the deck of a ocean liner, where nothing seems to change except the light and the cloud patterns in the sky overhead.

I began to notice the small streams trickling through culverts beneath the road. The water ran brown and muddy in treeless channels beneath the clear skies, frequently disappearing from sight beneath cornstalks planted to water's edge. Occasionally we crossed a larger stream, perhaps a river, where a few scraggly trees remained alongside the levees, which crowded the riverbanks to make still more space for cornfields.

Iowa, I realized, is an example of rural sprawl, or more accurately, agricultural sprawl—a landscape obliterated by corn and soybeans. Iowa farmlands, in their preemptive character, are comparable to Los Angeles or Atlanta or Phoenix, cities that have effectively erased their presettlement natural history.

On the seventh day we reached Muscatine on the Mississippi and wheeled our bikes down to the water to mark a pilgrimage completed. By then I had listened to many good stories about previous generations on the land, the history of homesteading, and the travails of the Great Depression. And I was beginning to assemble a clearer mental picture of what had been on this land before it was traumatized and subdued by the plow.

Tallgrass prairie once extended across the entire state, interspersed with oak savannas along streams that drained west to the Missouri and east to the Mississippi. In the center of the state, small lakes, potholes, and swamps dotted the land, occupying imperfectly drained soils, still fresh from the glaciers that had melted away little more than ten thousand years ago. Herds of bison had roamed the prairie, trailed by packs of wolves. Overhead, flocks of waterfowl had filled the skies, migrating south in the winter, returning in the spring to nest and breed on the waters.

Then the homesteaders arrived, migrating in from the Ohio Valley, the Appalachians, New England, and from countries across the sea; they broke sod, plowed, and planted, transforming the tallgrass prairie into the most productive agricultural land in the world. As the prairie disappeared, no one gave much thought to what was being lost; the prairie seemed limitless and there would always be more on the western horizon. By the end of the nineteenth century more than 99 percent of the tallgrass prairie of Iowa and the other midwestern states had vanished, replaced by row crops.

Only in recent times have we begun to tally the costs of this transformation from prairie to industrial agriculture. The bison herds are gone with the prairie that nourished them; the migratory waterfowl have declined as their nesting habitat disappeared. The loss of topsoil continues, relentlessly stripped away from exposed fields by wind and water. The Iowa Department of Agriculture, hardly an alarmist source, reports that fully half of the state's soil has been depleted, eroded by streams and carried away by wind, after fewer than two hundred years of farming. The Dust Bowl of the 1930s, now fading from contemporary memory, remains a reminder of what can happen when farmers ignore the limits imposed by climate and rainfall.

Water contamination is a serious threat, born of the vast increase in the use of ammonia-based fertilizers and pesticides since World War II. Water pollution threatens the groundwater on which farmers rely for domestic use. And the problem does not stop there. Fertilizers and pesticides dissolving in the rain and washing downstream and into the Gulf of Mexico a thousand miles away have begun to destroy ocean fisheries. A giant dead zone now spreads outward from the Mississippi Delta and westward along the Texas Gulf over an area the size of Massachusetts. The lesson is clear:

industrial agriculture has been extended too far, and the price has been too high for the land and waters to bear.

Some ten years after that first cycling trip across Iowa, I returned to the state, invited by local environmental leaders. Not without reason they believed that the secretary of the interior, like his predecessors, had ignored the state as lacking places worth preserving. Once on the ground in Des Moines I began to see a rather different reality. I listened to citizens who were inventorying remaining fragments of the tallgrass prairie, discovering remaining bits and pieces along railroad rights-of-way, in long forgotten cemeteries, in gullies, and on hillsides too steep to plow.

Then with local representatives of The Nature Conservancy I made a field trip to Council Bluffs, where that long-ago bike ride had started, this time to visit the Loess Hills, one of the best remaining fragments of the tallgrass prairie. These hills are a geological oddity, composed of windblown dust deposited as the glaciers of the last ice age retreated and since eroded into a network of ridges and gullies. Thus it is that the finest remaining tallgrass was still there for us to visit, saved from the plow by two natural adversaries — a vast and ancient dust bowl and a cycle of prolonged erosion.

Hiking through these hills, I saw for the first time the real thing, the fabled tallgrass: big bluestem, little bluestem, sand bluestem, Indian grass, and switchgrass rippling in the breeze, stems shooting up seven feet high, closing over my head. In the breaks leading toward the river, the slopes were studded with large oaks and hickories, interspersed with swatches of brilliant prairie flowers.

We paused on the crest of a hill to discuss how it had come to this — virtually nothing left, less than one-tenth of a percent of the tallgrass that had covered more than 85 percent of the state. Why hadn't something been done to preserve some of this landscape before it had disappeared? Were there no Iowa counterparts to the nineteenth-century conservation leaders who had worked so successfully to preserve the Adirondacks in New York and to establish a national forest system and our great national parks like Yellowstone and Yosemite?

The main reason for this neglect, we agreed, was that most visitors, then as now, didn't see much that merited saving in Iowa or most anywhere else in the Midwest. In the nineteenth century, Americans perceived landscapes by reference to a European literary and artistic tradition centered on sublime alpine scenery. Seeking out grand scenery in this European tradition, scientists, artists, illustrators, and writers—including the vanguard of the conservation movement—traveled, unseeing and uninterested, right on across the plains toward the spectacular vistas of the Rocky Mountains and the Sierra Nevada. A few paused to lament the disappearance of the bison and the plains Indians, but never long enough to advocate preservation of the midwestern landscapes.

In my visit to the Loess Hills, however, I began to learn of a generation of conservation activists who plan to resurrect and restore samples of the tallgrass prairie, working with scattered tracts of land, mostly a hundred acres or less in size. And work it is, for a tallgrass prairie, consisting of hundreds of species, is comparable in complexity to an old-growth forest, and not much less difficult to restore to its original ecological condition. Throughout the Midwest volunteers and scientists have been learning by doing, collecting native seeds, transplanting sod, releasing pollinators, and gradually beginning to re-create the complex assemblages of long-forgotten grasses, forbs, and flowers of the tallgrass prairie.

In 1991 Des Moines activists persuaded their congressman, Neal Smith, to obtain federal funding to purchase five thousand acres of cornfields near the city on which to establish a national wildlife refuge. It was, I thought, the first I had ever heard of a wildlife refuge without wildlife; but that, after all, is what a field of dreams is all about. The Fish and Wildlife Service is now working to bring back native prairie species, including a small herd of bison, in the Neal Smith National Wildlife Refuge.

Prairie restoration is also taking hold in other midwestern states. Illinois, "the prairie state," may have the most unusual restoration site — a five-hundred-acre plot located on the Fermi National Accelerator Laboratory, a nuclear research facility near Batavia. In 1996 President Clinton signed legislation creating the Midewin National Tallgrass Prairie, consisting of nearly twenty thousand acres at the deactivated Joliet Army Ammunition Plant south of Chicago. And Illinois even has a Web site listing the best rural cemeteries for seeing only slightly disturbed fragments of the original prairie.

Encountering the beginnings of yet another regional restoration movement, I wondered aloud about the larger, overarching vision. How did all these scattered projects add up? Were they just an opportunistic collection of sites, hinting at what has been lost but too small for true restoration? Or was there a larger vision of what might be accomplished within this generation? How much of that vanished 99 percent could we fairly reclaim for the wild? How much was necessary for functioning wetlands, what minimum size would be needed for a restored prairie ecosystem with enough space for free-ranging bison and their predators, for periodic renewal by wildfire, for streams running free, meandering and overflowing into their natural floodplains? Shouldn't agricultural spaces, like cities, be set in and balanced with natural space that supports wildlife, provides clear streams, and retains the ecological functioning of the land? Discussion was lively, but before we got very far it was time to leave the Loess Hills and return to Des Moines.

SINCE THAT MID-1990s trip, I have occasionally returned to Iowa in search of answers to those questions, comparing what I see to other agricultural regions of the country, looking for similarities and differences, seeking reference points for the ideal mix of farms, prairie, forest, and river valley — landscapes capable of sustaining ecosystems while continuing to support farmers and consumers here and around the world.

The first comparison that came to mind was the Central Valley of California, the region mainly responsible for ranking California first in agricultural production. Unhappily, the Central Valley has also been devastated by the overextension of agriculture, to the near elimination of wetlands and the destruction of entire rivers. Elsewhere I saw more hopeful patterns — the retained matrix of forests, meadows, and natural watercourses in many parts of New England, the Willamette Valley of Oregon, the Piedmont region east of the Appalachians, the Ohio River valley, and parts of the South. The unifying feature of these landscapes, for all their differences, is that many streams still run clear, through natural floodplains that retain their forest cover.

The beginning of a restoration vision starts with retaining and restoring these riparian patterns, the networks of rivers and streams that branch outward across the land like the veins on a tree leaf. The restoration of stream bottoms would take the marginal, flood-threatened lands out of production, would provide interconnected corridors for wildlife, and would make a major contribution toward restoring the degraded quality of our rivers, a subject discussed in the next chapter.

Beyond restoring the river networks, large blocks of land should be set aside to provide functional upland prairie expanses. The size and location of such spaces should take into account local, site-specific scientific, economic, and political considerations. In other parts of the world, especially in the tropics where much research had been concentrated, ecologists have concluded that, at least as a beginning rule of thumb, ecosystems can retain much of their natural function by keeping as little as 20 percent of the land in natural habitat. Given the chronic overproduction in midwestern agriculture, this seems an achievable target, one that would maintain farm income, benefit the land, and, as we shall see, have a less destructive impact on world agricultural prices.

In Iowa and the Midwest the quest for a larger restoration vision necessarily begins with an excursion into federal farm policy, that vast compendium of subsidies, price supports, export credits, and extension programs that influence every aspect of agriculture in the farm belt, shaping both the economics of farming and use of the land. The farm belt is one region where the debate about land use planning has long been settled, with farmers advocating a strong federal presence. As elsewhere federal policy in farm country has historically favored development, causing expansion of farming onto marginal lands, with attendant environmental destruction. Federal policy, however, is beginning a perceptible shift toward conservation land use planning, a trend that has enormous, not yet widely appreciated consequences for broad-scale environmental restoration in the Midwest, and indeed in many other regions of the country.

The federal ascendancy over farm policy began with the Farm Loan Act of 1916, which provided low-interest loans to assist farmers through an agricultural recession. It accelerated with price-guarantee programs to stimulate production during World War I. Then, as a prolonged agricultural recession settled across the farm belt after that war, farm organizations again turned to Congress, arguing that farmers should have incomes on a "parity" with the rest of American society. With the coming of the New Deal, the parity concept caught on and Congress began enacting legislation to raise commodity prices, both limiting production by imposing acreage restrictions and raising incomes by guaranteeing farmers a preset price to be paid by the government if market prices fell below the established targets.

In the intervening years programs to raise prices by limiting production have taken many forms: slaughtering livestock, taking acreage out of production on a year-to-year basis, and one all but forgotten program that could actually instruct future farm policy reform. In the Dust Bowl years, as drought and high winds combined to suck up huge clouds of topsoil and move it across the country, showering grit on the national capital and coating the decks of ships halfway across the Atlantic, Congress authorized the secretary of agriculture to purchase failed homesteads on the High Plains and to consolidate them into a system of national grasslands. By the time the program came to an end, sixteen such areas totaling more four million acres had been established, setting an important, if little-known precedent for the establishment of permanent conservation lands.

But the dominant policies have been price supports and acreage restrictions. For all the tinkering and experimentation, these two contradictory policies — the one a stimulus to production, the other designed to *reduce* production and thus supply — have remained at war with each other, complicating farm policy to the present day.

The price supports established by the New Deal have evolved into a complex of programs under which the Department of Agriculture pays the farmer a subsidy when the market price for which the crop is sold falls below a preset target level. In 2004 when corn sold on the market for $1.91 per bushel, participating farmers became eligible for a government payment of $0.24 per bushel. There are of course many variations on this basic concept, and if a quarter a bushel seems like a small amount, the total spent on farm programs of all kinds every year averages more than fifteen billion dollars. Willie Nelson, it seems, did not invent farm aid.

This deficiency payment program, however necessary it may be to smooth out the unpredictable weather-driven fluctuations in farm production and variations in market demand, has the obvious defect of encouraging farmers to put more land into production. This often means moving onto previously bypassed marginal land in forested river floodplains, prairie potholes, and hillsides easily subject to erosion.

And these deficiency payments, however beneficial to the individual farmer, also have economic implications for the rest of the world. More production, as a general rule, will lower market prices, triggering higher subsidy payments, which stimulate still more production. The losers are farmers in Africa and other developing countries who cannot compete with subsidized exports from countries like the United States.

In 1985 Congress took a step to control overproduction by enacting a new acreage-reduction scheme called the Conservation Reserve Program, which has the most conservation potential of any program since the national grasslands initiative of the Great Depression years. The CRP encourages farmers to reduce production by offering payments to take land out of production and plant it in grass or other perennial cover to reduce erosion. Since farmers are paid about the same amount of money as they would net from farming the land, the program has won wide acceptance. Unlike deficiency payments, the CRP land-rental payments do not have the adverse economic effect of stimulating production; in fact they do just the opposite. The CRP payment, in the language of economists, is uncoupled from production, an incentive to grow less rather than more.

By requiring that farmers plant grass or other perennial cover to protect the soil from erosion, the program also takes a small first step toward a big new idea — that farmers can be paid, not just to curtail production, but also to manage the land toward conservation objectives. That said, the CRP as currently administered has added relatively little to the restoration side of the ledger. Landowners retain the right to withdraw from the program when their contracts expire and to restart production whenever commodity prices rise sufficiently to provide the possibility of a better return than that offered by the CRP payments. This in and out policy precludes genuine restoration. Tallgrass prairie and forested stream buffers take time to develop; they cannot be planted one year, then plowed under a few years later as if they were just another crop. Further diminishing conservation value, farmers are allowed to plant non-native grasses that have little wildlife value and have the potential to spread out of control. And farmers remain largely free to enroll land in the program in scattered bits and pieces that do not necessarily further conservation goals such as establishing connectivity or providing stream buffers.

Nonetheless the CRP remains an important precedent, establishing the concept that farmers can appropriately receive income for taking steps to restore the land. It is a precedent with potential to shape a revolution in farm policy, combining meaningful restoration programs and a means to save the farm economy from an oncoming political crisis. For when the farm bill comes up for reauthorization in 2007, there will be a new and unfamiliar participant on the field — the World Trade Organization.

FOR OUR PURPOSES the trade story begins in 2003 in the city of Doha in Qatar, where the member countries of the World Trade Organization gathered to take up the subject of trade in agricultural products. Agriculture is a sector in which free trade principles have long been ignored by the United States, Japan, and the European countries that have traditionally dominated international trade negotiations. This double standard, in which we advocate free trade for high technology, manufactures, and intellectual property while protecting our agricultural sector, is not unique; it is part of a pattern among all advanced democracies in which countries with the means to do so routinely protect and subsidize their politically powerful farm sectors.

In the past, the developing countries — victims of these practices — have been too disorganized and lacking in economic and political sophistication to fight back. At Doha, however, these countries began to speak up. African countries, led by Sierra Leone and Niger, complained bitterly that the dumping of subsidized American cotton prevents their farmers from producing cotton that could otherwise be competitive in world markets. Brazil and other soybean producers alleged that American soybean subsidies give American farmers an incentive to dump their products on the world market, artificially depressing world prices and injuring soybean farmers in other countries. The Caribbean countries and other tropical sugar producers voiced similar complaints with respect to sugar. At Doha the developing countries, having discovered an international forum for their common interests, refused to bargain about their protection for manufactured goods, high tech, and intellectual property without progress on agriculture. With few concessions forthcoming from the developed countries, the talks collapsed.

The following year, in 2004, at a follow-on session in Cancun, this newly invigorated block of developing countries—with leadership and support from countries too big to ignore, including Brazil, India, and China—renewed their demands for concessions on agricultural subsidies from the United States and other industrialized nations. Once again the talks collapsed. Observers sympathetic to the United States pointed out that the talks were taking place in the year of a presidential election, hardly a time to expect concessions sure to stir controversy in the farm belt.

In the meantime Brazil, dissatisfied with the pace of progress, filed a complaint with the WTO alleging that American cotton subsidies have become so excessive as to violate existing trade agreements, which do allow some cotton subsidies in the interim before permanent rules can be established. In the summer of 2004 a WTO arbitration panel entered a preliminary ruling in favor of Brazil, placing still more pressure on the United States and the European Union.

The resolution of these conflicts will undoubtedly be years in the making, but the handwriting is on the wall. The United States, deeply committed to the principles of free trade, historically the world leader in advocating open markets as the pathway to economic development, transparency and democracy, and ultimately as an antidote to terrorism, must now get in formation and begin marching to the beat of its own drummer. And in the absence of progress the United States will face possible penalties from the WTO and retaliation from other countries that could lead to disastrous trade wars. Congress will have to move, however reluctantly, to begin dismantling the agricultural subsidies that violate free trade principles. And the program of deficiency payments will be at the top of the list.

This impending, inevitable change in the economic underpinnings of American agriculture opens up an unprecedented opportunity to implement regional programs of environmental restoration in a manner consistent with trade rules even while retaining income security for farmers. Farm payments, uncoupled from production, can provide the means to permanently retire lands from production and to dedicate them to the restoration of tallgrass prairie, streams, and wetlands. This opportunity will become available, not just in Iowa and the rest of the Midwest, but in every region of the country where agriculture is supported by federal production subsidies. That includes the Atlantic coast regions and southern states, which also grow corn and soybeans. It takes in the arid High Plains that extend westward from the corn belt to the foot of the Rocky Mountains where wheat is grown. And it includes the irrigated, cotton-growing valleys of California and southern Arizona.

How might this transformation work in practice? The first step will be to comply with developing WTO agriculture rules by dismantling the trade-distorting deficiency payments that are calculated based on acres farmed. Congress will then have a choice: either abolish subsidies altogether or construct an alternative income-support program that does not violate free trade rules.

The Heritage Foundation, the Cato Institute, and other libertarian think tanks see this transformation as a chance to abolish price supports and other agricultural subsidies, casting farmers out to sink or swim in the currents of the free market. That is not likely to happen, though. Even with budget deficits and pressure to cut domestic spending, agricultural subsidies have become a way of life. Farmers may constitute less than 2 percent of the American work force, but they have the tradition of Thomas Jefferson's yeoman farmer and the enduring image of the family farm on their side, to say nothing of a representational system, which guarantees that sparsely populated farm states continue to be overrepresented in the U.S. Senate.

If farm subsidies are not going to disappear, and if the WTO is not going to vanish, there will have to be a middle ground that embodies both objectives: eliminating trade distortions and continuing to provide income support to struggling farmers. One way out would be to decouple farm payments from crop production, substituting direct payments to which farmers would be entitled simply for being farmers, regardless of annual acres in production.

As attractive as this may sound as a means of complying with free trade principles, the notion of recasting farm subsidies in the form of direct, uncoupled payments carries the risk that farm assistance will be further stigmatized, as just another form of welfare. If farmers are to receive payments simply for owning a piece of farmland, how is that different from young mothers on welfare or assistance to the elderly and disabled? You should not, the argument goes, pay farmers for idling the farm and taking a holiday in Florida. Even welfare recipients have work requirements.

So if Congress remains unwilling to eliminate farm subsidies, and if a program of outright uncoupled cash payments is unacceptable, the search for a third way will come down to establishing some "farm nexus," some service or work requirement rendered in exchange for receiving federal assistance that does not violate the developing rules of free trade. Such a WTO-compliant farm nexus could consist of engaging landowners in a comprehensive program of land and water restoration as a condition of federal aid.

As is often the case, if one looks carefully through history, helpful precedents for designing new programs emerge. Take the case of duck hunters. More than half of all the migratory ducks in North America breed in the spring in the prairie pothole region of the upper Midwest, in the states of Minnesota, North Dakota, South Dakota, Iowa, and Montana. Prairie potholes are small, shallow lakes that fill depressions left by melting glaciers of the last ice age. This wetland region is known as the "duck factory," for each year it sends forth millions of migratory birds to the lower Mississippi River valley and the Gulf coast, where duck hunting generates big money in many rural economies.

Migratory waterfowl populations have always fluctuated in response to drought and rainfall conditions in the upper Midwest, but in the 1960s the duck populations began a steady long-term decline, as farmers seeking to expand production began draining and plowing the prairie potholes. Led by a hunter group, Ducks Unlimited, conservationists descended on Congress to make an appealing argument: if farmers are getting subsidies from the American taxpayer, they should at least be required to stop plowing up prairie potholes. In response Congress enacted the so-called swampbuster provision, which made farmers who continued to plow up prairie potholes ineligible for deficiency payments or other subsidies.

Duck hunters and conservationists then lobbied for an affirmative program to restore prairie potholes that had been lost to farming. The result was the Wetlands Reserve Program, where instead of receiving a crop subsidy, a farmer would be paid to quit farming a relevant parcel of land, restoring it instead to wetland habitat.

Under the law a farmer can enter into a ten-year contract, or give a fifteen-year conservation easement, or even sell a permanent easement while retaining possession the land. This program, together with land set-asides under the Conservation Reserve Program, has to date restored several million acres of the upper Midwest to migratory waterfowl habitat. And since these programs were initiated, average annual migratory waterfowl populations have increased by more than 25 percent.

The success of the Wetlands Reserve Program can be attributed to several factors: the articulation of a measurable conservation objective (increasing the populations of migratory waterfowl); an effective swampbuster prohibition against destruction of wetland habitat; and the targeted selection of lands to conserve and restore based on their importance as waterfowl habitat.

The prairie pothole region of the upper Midwest includes something less than 10 percent of the nation's agricultural lands that produce federally subsidized crops such as corn, soybeans, sorghum, peanuts, wheat, and cotton. It is now time to formulate effective restoration programs for these other regions as well. And the place to begin is with the conservation reserve idea. In its present form, as noted earlier, this program allows the planting of ecologically inappropriate cover crops for limited periods of time. It thus provides little or no incentive for the development of enduring restoration values. It does, however, contain conceptual seeds that could be made to blossom into a genuine restoration program.

To expand the CRP into a meaningful program of comprehensive restoration will require three basic changes. First, the CRP's flaw of allowing farmers to take land in and out of the program makes long term, permanent restoration virtually impossible. The basic irreducible requirement for a new program must be that designated lands will be retired for permanent prairie and watershed restoration.

Second, the CRP and related programs are shot through with

loopholes that allow creative farmers to collect CRP payments on one portion of their land while simultaneously plowing up new land in order to continue collecting an undiminished, or even increased, level of production-based deficiency payments—a situation that could actually result in a net loss for conservation. That loophole should be closed and sealed.

A third defect, probably in greatest need of change, is the CRP's failure to define restoration objectives that will clearly identify lands to be taken out of production and dedicated to restoration. When lands are selected in the current random fashion, mostly at the discretion and convenience of the landowner, there is little hope for effective, permanent restoration of streams, wetlands, and wildlife habitat necessary for overall health of the land. Natural ecosystems require connected spaces, not detached fragments. Throughout the Midwest I have walked through corn and soybean fields where scattered tracts in the center were enrolled in the CRP while environmentally significant lands bordering streams and rivers remained in corn and soybeans right up to the water's edge.

The prerequisite for comprehensive restoration of a region is to define objectives and to map out the spaces that should be withdrawn from farming and returned to their natural state. There is no preset formula for establishing an appropriate balance between row-crop farming and the restoration of wild places; the process will inevitably involve the exercise of judgment informed by careful science and thoughtful attention to the economic realities of farming.

We can begin this process by consulting the land itself. In the words of Job, "Ask now the beasts, and they shall teach thee; and the fowls of the air, and they shall teach thee; or speak to the earth and it shall teach thee." The birds and the beasts do not read maps, and streams do not cease flowing at property boundaries; restoring the streams and river floodplains that provide connectivity is the first step in restoring the land's ecological functions.

Upgrading and transforming the CRP will require two additional changes. First, the process of defining objectives and drawing maps should be expanded into a collaborative federal-state-landowner process. Ironically, states at present are largely absent from the discussion, a testament to how thoroughly farm programs have been federalized. And second, following the example set by the swampbuster legislation, farm aid should always be conditioned on participation in restoration programs.

In 2004 the senior editor of the *Des Moines Register* wrote a column urging his readers to begin thinking of Iowa, not as the tall-corn state, but as the tallgrass prairie state:

"Not so long ago," he wrote, "the Florida Everglades were regarded much as Iowa prairies were — as useless wasteland. The imperative was to drain them so the land could be used for other purposes. Now the government is spending hundreds of millions of dollars to bring back the Everglades, which are recognized as a priceless ecological asset to the state.

"So it should be with the tallgrass prairie in Iowa."

The transformation of the Everglades from dismal swamp to national treasure did not occur overnight. All along the way it was aided by grassroots support and by the application of modern ecological science that persuaded the public that, to save the Everglades National Park, you had to restore the ecosystem surrounding it by reconnecting the entire watershed.

These same concepts can also inform large-scale restoration projects in the Midwest. And in one respect, at least, the task should be easier to accomplish; in the farm belt, the money for restoration is already in the federal budget — lying dormant within that fifteen-billion-dollar farm program account. All that remains is to persuade the region's farmers and the American public that, as farm assistance programs are transformed to meet the requirements of the global economy, it will be in farmers' interests to embrace a visionary program of regional restoration.

4

At Water's Edge

SOME TIME AGO, on my way from western Maryland back to Washington, I noticed a sign on Interstate 70 that read, "Entering the Chesapeake Bay Watershed." It seemed just another of those ubiquitous "entering" and "leaving" road signs erected across the country by service clubs, civic boosters, and local officials. A week later, returning from central Virginia, I saw a similar sign just south of the Rappahannock River. This time the sign made me think of the condition of the bay itself and all that I had read about the decline of the fisheries there. Then I saw another sign along Interstate 81 in the Shenandoah Valley, and I finally got the message: the waters in the bay were in trouble because of what was happening out here on the land. The collapse of the fisheries in the bay was a land use problem that extended throughout the watershed into six states—New York, Pennsylvania, West Virginia, Virginia, Maryland, and Delaware—all the land up to the crest line of the Appalachians.

For years I had seen and heard news accounts of the decline of Chesapeake Bay—and of mayors and governors holding summit meetings, then issuing press releases pledging mutual cooperation and calling for voluntary action to prevent and clean up the waste discharges and runoff polluting the bay. But as secretary of the interior I didn't pay as much attention as I might have because the bay's problems were primarily water quality problems. They fell within the jurisdiction of the Environmental Protection Agency, which administered the Clean Water Act. My primary task was land management, and I tended to regard the two—land and water—as separate in fact and in law. While seldom reticent about transgressing bureaucratic jurisdictional lines, I just did not see Chesapeake Bay as a priority for my department. These highway signs reminded me that I should have done more to bring public attention to that connection. To restore our rivers and estuaries we must manage the land, taking full account of the hydrologic cycle, a lesson as ancient as the words of Ecclesiastes: "All streams flow into the sea, yet the sea is not full. To the place the streams come from, there they return again."

Like so many of our natural resources, the bay once seemed inexhaustible, its waters so vast and productive as to be beyond serious harm. Oyster reefs were so extensive they were mapped and marked as hazards on navigation charts. Blue crabs swarmed through huge fields of sea grass that covered the shallows, and spawning shad, herring, and striped bass crowded rivers flowing into the bay.

The founding fathers were dining on Chesapeake oysters as they drafted the Constitution in nearby Philadelphia. As farmers moved inland clearing the forests and plowing the land, the bay, unchanged, continued to produce prodigious amounts of seafood. As the industrial revolution accelerated, Chesapeake oysters, packed in the newly invented tin can, appeared in cities throughout the nation. By the end of the nineteenth century the bay produced more that 20 percent of the seafood consumed in the entire country.

Then in about 1950, after centuries of production, the fisheries began to collapse. The oyster harvest, once more than thirty million bushels per season, declined to a mere twenty-five thousand bushels. The live oyster reefs crumbled into heaps of decaying shells. The beds of sea grass began to die off, shrinking to less than a third of their original expanse. On the hottest days of summer, crabs began crawling ashore to avoid suffocation in oxygen-depleted bottom waters. The striped bass are today so contaminated with PCBs that Maryland advises limiting intake to less than twice a month for adults and even less frequently for children. Thousands of watermen have joined the ranks of the unemployed, their shoreline communities lined with rusting skipjacks and empty packing sheds.

Scientists studying the bay discerned a now familiar pattern: most ecological systems are quite robust and are capable of withstanding considerable stress from pollution and overharvesting, up to a point when the cumulative effects trigger a sudden, sometimes irreversible collapse of the system. Seeking the causes of decline, researchers focused initially on industrial discharges and untreated sewage pouring into the bay from nearby cities. Then in 1972 the Clean Water Act was signed into law with stringent provisions mandating industries to reduce and ultimately eliminate most discharges, and requiring cities to treat and disinfect their sewage. The act established a framework for the Environmental Protection Agency to set pollution standards; and it then required industries and cities to obtain permits, setting timetables for cleanup. The legislation also invited the states into a partnership to administer the act, providing financial assistance and giving generous construction grants for municipal sewage treatment plants to jump-start the process of compliance.

These "point source" controls proved effective, but the life systems of the bay did not seem to respond and initial high expectations for a quick recovery soon faded. The oyster reefs virtually disappeared. Crab fisheries continued to decline. Gradually a more complex picture emerged as scientists discovered that, with industrial and municipal discharges coming under control, land use throughout the six-state watershed was now the largest contributor to the pollution killing the bay.

Studies then pointed toward three suspect contaminants: nitrogen, phosphorus, and a somewhat surprising third element—sediment, just plain ordinary dirt. The quantities of nitrogen and phosphorus washing into the bay spiked sharply in the years after World War II, not coincidentally at the very time that petrochemical fertilizers came into widespread use. Farmers quickly discovered that application of chemical fertilizers containing these two elements, essential to plant growth, greatly increased yields of corn and soybeans. Chemical fertilizers are relatively inexpensive, and to avoid the risk of using too little, farmers routinely used too much. Fertilizers are also highly soluble, and whatever was not taken up by the crops dissolved in the runoff from every rainstorm, flowing into creeks and rivers and eventually into the bay.

Added to the Chesapeake Bay waters, these elements continued to fertilize, stimulating the growth of algae, which spread in huge blooms that blocked sunlight and deprived the sea grasses of photosynthetic energy. As the algal blooms died off, they rained down on the bottom, where they decomposed, taking up dissolved oxygen and rendering the waters uninhabitable to many forms of sea life, including the blue crabs crawling ashore to avoid suffocation. Nutrient on the land, fertilizer became poison in the waters of the bay, just as is occurring off the mouth of the Mississippi River in the Gulf of Mexico as a result of farming practices throughout the Midwest.

As for sediment, anyone could see what was happening by driving through the farmlands extending back from the shores of Chesapeake Bay, where freshly plowed fields lay exposed to the rain, bleeding sediment into the creeks, which then coalesced into torrents of muddy water flowing into the bay. Spreading across the bay, the sediment clouded the water, starving the sea grasses of essential sunlight.

THE AUTHORS OF the Clean Water Act recognized that our waters could not be restored without action to control the widespread runoff that constitutes "non–point source" pollution. But they could not agree on what to do about it. Direct federal regulation of millions of landowners through a permit system analogous to that imposed upon municipal and industrial point sources seemed out of the question. And for whatever reason, the authors of the Clean Water Act seemed disinclined to grapple with providing a system of meaningful incentives to induce state action. So, in the end, the legislation simply passed the problem on to the states, with vague language suggesting they should adopt non–point source pollution control plans.

What the federal government was unwilling to do, the states proved even less willing to attempt. In the more than thirty years since the Clean Water Act was enacted, no state yet has produced a meaningful plan to clean up and restore its waters by managing land uses. A handful of states, prodded by litigation, have taken preliminary steps to assess their watersheds, to propose standards intended to prevent further degradation, and to assign tentative quotas for the reduction of pollution, all through an elaborate standard-setting process known as TMDL (the allowable Total Maximum Daily Load of pollution). Still, after thirty years no state has managed to implement an effective program to halt stream degradation resulting from land use or to begin the process of cleaning up the waters by managing the way land is used. Today more than half the nation's waters still do not meet the "fishable, swimmable" goal set forth in the Clean Water Act.

For all this history of procrastination and foot dragging, the Clean Water Act may yet play an important role in comprehensive land use planning. The act has both the narrow focus and broad reach appropriate to a federal land use statute. It treats only matters of essential national concern, relating to the protection and restoration of our rivers, lakes, and wetlands, by prescribing measures to manage land use that degrades those waters. It does not speak to "land use planning" in the more traditional sense of the phrase, that is, to the fine-grained local decisions such as where to locate an airport, to run power lines, or to place aggregate pits, or to matters involving the relative locations of industrial zones, commercial establishments, and subdivisions—issues properly left to state and local decision. What the non–point source provision of the Clean Water Act does address is what is, or should be, an important federal concern, to which much of this book is addressed: the protection and restoration on a large scale of our natural landscapes and ecosystems.

The principal reason for the failure of the Clean Water Act at this landscape scale lies in the failure to implement a workable federal-state regulatory partnership. Generally speaking, Congress cannot order a state legislature to pass a law or adopt a plan. But Congress can devise an appropriate mix of incentives and sanctions designed to induce public support and state action, something yet to be attained in the administration of the Clean Water Act's land use provisions.

To imagine how such incentives might work requires separate consideration of the two major land use practices affected by the Clean Water Act: first, management of agricultural lands, and second, urban sprawl onto "greenfield" sites (agricultural land or open space as distinct from "brownfield" sites, which have already been in industrial use).

Farming is the most widespread and least regulated land use affecting our aquatic ecosystems. More than 60 percent of the lands within the watershed of the Mississippi-Missouri river system, which gathers waters from thirty-two states, is planted to crops, including corn, soybeans, wheat, and alfalfa. The land is rich and productive, and farmers, encouraged by federal agriculture policies, have continually expanded at the expense of natural grassland and forest cover. Federal policy has encouraged and subsidized this process; one agriculture secretary in the Nixon administration is remembered for repeatedly urging farmers to plant "fencerow to fencerow."

The result of these maximum production, nature-annihilating practices, as we saw in the preceding chapter, is most evident in the flat expanses of Iowa and southern Illinois where rectangular fields march from horizon to horizon, uninterrupted by any natural cover other than scraps of prairie grass in old cemeteries and the clumps of trees that shade the farmhouses. The streams, stripped of tree canopies and planted to water's edge, run thick and muddy. The land has been transformed into an industrial landscape, from which natural features, wetlands, forest patches, and wildlife have been largely obliterated.

Proper application of the Clean Water Act could bring these regions back to balance with only minimal adjustments in land use. Muddy creeks and sloughs can be restored by simply bringing back the natural canopy to river bottoms and bordering fields with vegetated strips to trap sediment and soak up dissolved fertilizer nutrients. Creating a more diverse landscape by restoring natural patterns of streams and rivers would draw wildlife back to land, provide clear and clean water, restore downstream fisheries, and begin the process of reviving our bays and estuaries.

The key to restoring farm landscapes, which will lead to renewal of our waters, is to establish a mixture of regulatory requirements and economic incentives sufficient to induce states to adopt restoration plans and farmers to comply with them. The necessary incentives can be established by conditioning income support on implementing restoration measures essential to the functioning of natural systems, as outlined in the previous chapter.

The Clean Water Act also has important, largely unrealized implications for land development and sprawl containment. New development on virgin land generates large volumes of uncontrolled stormwater runoff from roofs, sidewalks, and streets. Water is a powerful solvent, and runoff picks up oil and metal residue from streets, lawn pesticides, animal waste, and septic discharges, moving all of these contaminants into groundwater and into surface streams.

Properly implemented, water-quality standards would require developers to incur the costs of installing facilities to treat both sewage and stormwater runoff and, where needed, to protect pristine streams further by retaining and reusing all treated effluent within the boundaries of their developments. These measures, by internalizing the true environmental costs of greenfield development, would not of themselves prohibit sprawl. They should, however, by making greenfield development more costly, induce both builders and buyers to consider new housing within existing urban boundaries, where infrastructure and water-treatment facilities are already in place.

As with agriculture the question is how to devise the proper mix of regulatory measures and economic incentives to induce states to adopt regulations that will translate into cooperation from builders and buyers. Some federal programs already in existence actually suggest how this might be accomplished. In 1968 Congress established a national program of flood insurance designed to compensate homeowners for losses from infrequent but highly destructive floods that were not adequately covered by conventional homeowner insurance and underwriting practices. This insurance, however, was and is available only to homeowners in communities that have enacted flood plain regulations that meet federal standards.

The law has since won widespread acceptance and has demonstrably reduced development in river bottoms, a nice illustration of how a federal incentive can produce far-reaching change in state and local land use plans. The concept behind this insurance program could readily be extended to provide incentives for states to manage sprawl development, for example by denying federal flood insurance to greenfield developments that do not meet enhanced standards for the control of wastewater and stormwater runoff.

CONTROLLING POLLUTED RUNOFF, from both point and non–point sources, means managing water after use as it leaves the land and heads into rivers and ultimately the sea to begin the hydrologic cycle all over again. However, we too seldom consider the environmental implications at the front end of the cycle, at the point that water is diverted from streams, rivers, and lakes for delivery to municipal, agricultural, and industrial uses. The allocation and distribution of water can be a powerful tool for good land use planning, especially in regions where water supplies are limited. Consider the remarkable case of Los Angeles. Back in 1905 it was a small city of fewer than two hundred thousand inhabitants seemingly without much of a future. It had already outstripped its meager water supplies; the seasonal flow of the Los Angeles River had been used up, and the wells on the coastal plain were beginning to draw saltwater.

At that point concerned city leaders began looking clear across the state to the Owens River, on the lee side of the Sierra Nevada, wondering how they might tap that source for Los Angeles. The ensuing raid on the Owens Valley is now ensconced in history and legend as a prime example of how large, powerful urban centers use their political and financial power to further development at the expense of small, powerless rural communities.

Yet the Los Angeles experience can also be viewed from another perspective—as an instructive example of regional land use planning carried out through water allocation. By reaching out and seizing control of available water from the entire region, Los Angeles invented itself as the monopoly water provider, thereby guaranteeing that growth would be concentrated within the Los Angeles basin. In the movie *Chinatown*, Noah Cross, the unscrupulous character representing a composite of historical Los Angeles leaders, puts the matter succinctly: "Either you bring the water to L.A. or you bring L.A. to the water."

Had William Mulholland never emerged to orchestrate the water grab, and had the waters of the Owens River been more equitably distributed throughout the region among large and small communities, the landscapes of Southern California might be even more broken up by sprawling development than they are today. Mulholland was no Frederick Law Olmsted; nonetheless his strong-arm tactics could hardly have been better planned to delineate the broad outlines of separation between urban and rural on the California landscape.

This pattern of urbanization powered by monopoly control of water, pioneered by Los Angeles, was repeated throughout the West in the twentieth century, often furthered by federal leadership, commencing with the Reclamation Act of 1902. This legislation spawned the Bureau of Reclamation and provided both legal authority and a continuing stream of appropriations for "reclaiming" western lands for settlement by developing and allocating scarce water resources.

The Bureau, chartered as a water management agency, was equally a land use planning agency, for a time even surpassing the role played in other parts of the country by the Army Corps of Engineers. Arizona, an early focus of reclamation activity, provides an example. To develop water in that state, the Bureau first had to decide where the water was to be used on the land, which meant it had to create the equivalent of a state land use plan, setting in place development patterns that persist to this day.

In 1908 the Bureau initiated construction of Roosevelt Dam on the Salt River upstream and northeast of Phoenix. And it eventually followed with five more dams, built on the rivers that drain the highlands of northern and eastern Arizona, in the process appropriating the surface waters of the uplands for the benefit of one downstream region. Phoenix and the surrounding farmland, occupied by fewer than ten thousand residents in 1910, had been preemptively awarded the water resources of half the state, thereby assuring that it would become the urban center of Arizona. Today this early, federal-planned community is a metropolis of more than three and a half million, with more than 60 percent of the state's population.

Through its water decisions, the Bureau of Reclamation thus determined where future growth would occur and where, for lack of water, it could not occur on a large scale. Scores of small upstream communities, denied the use of nearby rivers, were consigned to a lesser future, looking on as their water flowed downstream into federal reservoirs built for the benefit of Phoenix and central Arizona.

Yet, by concentrating the water resources essential to development in a few selected places, federal planners and their state counterparts created an oasis model of development, consisting of a few well-watered centers surrounded by miles and miles of desert ranges and open upland forests. While the oasis itself hardly proved to be a model of urban planning, the grand, uncluttered surrounding expanses of desert and mountain are testimony to an effective regional landscape protection plan, the largely unintended result of federal water allocation policies.

This pattern of federal water allocation as a form of regional planning—centered around fueling the growth of existing urban centers to the perceived detriment of outlying communities—was extended to other western states. In New Mexico the Bureau of Reclamation assured the future of Albuquerque with a series of dams and diversion works that effectively appropriated a lion's share of the Rio Grande for that city's benefit.

And in Nevada the Bureau has allocated that state's entire share of the Colorado River to one urban area—Las Vegas. The result of this federally created water monopoly can be seen by any visitor to southern Nevada. Las Vegas is a giant urban oasis surrounded by desert expanses that are utterly vacant, without even the usual scattering of outlying wildcat subdivisions. Development simply stops where there is no water, and there is none outside the service areas of Las Vegas. Limited water service—combined with the urban boundaries effectively set in place by Senator Reid and the Endangered Species Act and with conservation designations on surrounding federal lands (see chapter 2)—has created a clear demarcation between urban and surrounding natural landscapes, in sharp contrast to the outward-sprawling, relentlessly merging cities of the well-watered Atlantic coast. Census statistics tell the story from another perspective: 70 percent of all Nevada residents live in one urban area, Las Vegas.

The land use and development patterns generated by these federally led water allocation policies have been a major factor in preserving the open landscapes and sense of space that is so distinctively western. The Colorado Plateau extends across large parts of four states, the quintessential western place of ancient cliff dwellings, red-rock canyons, mountains and mesas, national forests, and a dozen national parks. The land has remained remarkably open and intact, even as on the periphery the large cities of Denver, Salt Lake City, Albuquerque, Las Vegas, and Phoenix continue to expand. This oasis pattern concentrates human impacts in relatively small areas, leaving the surrounding landscapes largely undisturbed and interconnected. It is a landscape model suggestive of how we can order our presence on the land, concentrating development so as to preserve the very features that draw people to a region in the first instance.

This western experience of water-driven planning and settlement, with its centripetal, confining tendency toward urban centers in open landscapes, has significant, if more limited applications to other regions of the country. Cities in other regions typically do not emerge as scarcity-driven monopoly water providers, for developers and other landowners have alternatives; they can frequently access shallow groundwater aquifers beneath their own land. Nonetheless, cities, wherever located, could use their water resources more creatively than they typically do; water is a public resource that can be developed and allocated flexibly, with fewer legal and political constraints than apply to the zoning of private land. A landowner generally has no legal right to demand that the water service area of a municipality be extended outward to include his land. Yet municipalities have all too often, reflexively and unthinkingly, acted to extend water service, following and facilitating patterns of sprawl. And all too often the associated infrastructure costs of extending water service are paid through property taxes on existing development, thereby encouraging and subsidizing still more sprawling development.

Cities could instead take much more initiative in using water allocation to shape and limit sprawling expansion, and to promote infill. When water infrastructure is created with public money, it could be used to concentrate growth, to limit sprawl, and to delineate boundaries between the built environment and the natural landscape.

THE OASIS PATTERN of development is not without troublesome side effects, most of them plainly visible in the West. Urban residents, disconnected from the reality of the desert, use water as if it were an inexhaustible resource. Developments are landscaped to resemble Brazilian rain forests and partly as a result, per capita water use in urban areas of the arid West is considerably higher than elsewhere in the country. Everywhere in this country we are consuming too much water, and in the process drying up and destroying many of our streams, springs, lakes, and other aquatic ecosystems. This ecological damage incurred by the overappropriation of streams, rivers, and groundwater resources has gone largely unnoticed and unregulated.

Again, Los Angeles provides one of the earliest examples. The raid on Owens Valley, for all its development-concentrating benefits, was carried on without any restraint, taking water and then more water and more until none was left. The aquatic system of the valley was completely destroyed, the Owens River dried up, and its terminal lake reduced to a puddle. In Arizona the reclamation effort ultimately siphoned off so much water that it dried up the two-hundred-mile stretch of the Gila River below Phoenix, where the former river course is marked by expanses of gravel and the whitened skeletons of cottonwood trees. In New Mexico, Albuquerque's demand for water has dried up the lower reaches of the Rio Grande within that state. In California water diversions have dried up and destroyed the San Joaquin River, where salmon once spawned in the foothills of the Sierra Nevada.

Not even the Colorado River, the largest river in the Intermountain West, has been spared. The river delta, just across the border in Mexico at the head of the Sea of Cortez—once covered with thick forests of mesquite and cottonwood, interspersed with meander channels and backwaters, populated by waterfowl, deer, and jaguars—is now mostly a barren, featureless salt flat. The rivers of the Southwest, which western developers and irrigators like to refer to as "working rivers," have been worked to death.

The diminishment of the nation's aquatic ecosystems is by no means exclusively a western phenomenon; it is now spreading into the southern and eastern sections of the country. On the Gulf coast of Florida, the city of Tampa reached out to develop new well fields fifty miles inland in Hendry County, a rural area dotted with small lakes connected to and replenished by the shallow limestone aquifers typical of the Florida peninsula. Then as the pumping volume increased, the lakes began to disappear, reduced to soggy mudflats.

In Texas, San Antonio draws most of its water from the Edwards Aquifer, once considered an inexhaustible source of groundwater. Now, however, pumping threatens to dry up the great springs at Comal and New Braunfels, putting at risk several endangered minnow and plant species. In Georgia and Alabama, excess diversions from the Chattahoochee River may potentially disrupt the rich fisheries downstream in Apalachicola Bay. And even in Massachusetts, groundwater pumping by the City of Boston periodically dries up the Ipswich River.

With continuing droughts in some parts of the country and steadily increasing population growth, this pattern of environmental destruction driven by high water demand is likely to spread unless patterns of water extraction and use are modified by a combination of increased efficiency and adequate regulation of water withdrawals.

The destruction of aquatic resources is seen by some as, however lamentable, the inevitable price that must be paid for progress and development. Yet nothing could be further from the truth. Simple statistics easily refute notions of an insoluble water crisis, even in the arid regions of the West. Of the water used in the West, nearly 80 percent goes for agriculture, half of which could be saved with the use of modern irrigation technology (for example, by using drip irrigation instead of flooding entire fields). Of the urban uses, nearly 40 percent flows onto outdoor lawns and landscaping. Water has been treated as such a cheap, inexhaustible commodity that many cities and farms do not even meter or otherwise measure the amounts consumed. The destruction of rivers and aquatic ecosystems, so frequently and fatalistically accepted as the inevitable price of progress, turns out to be entirely unnecessary.

In its present form, the Clean Water Act does not speak directly to water quantity, what is used or what is left; it regulates only water quality and those who pollute it. While it is illegal to pollute a river, the Clean Water Act does not directly prevent you from destroying the river by diverting all the water. This is rather like a legal system that prohibits spraying graffiti on a building, yet says nothing about burning the structure to the ground.

Although the regulatory provisions of the Clean Water Act do not address depletion, the preamble to the act does recognize the issue, for it establishes as a goal the restoration of the physical, chemical, and biological integrity of the water resource. I believe it is time to expand the regulatory reach of the Clean Water Act to accomplish that goal by adding a provision to prohibit the depletion of streams and lakes below the level sufficient to sustain them as living resources. Such revision would require establishing a hydrologic "bright line" for sustaining streamflows, marking a share for the aquatic ecosystem below which rivers cannot be depleted.

What might that "bright line" level be? And who would make the determination? And how would it be enforced? Minimum stream-flow is not a new idea. On the Sacramento River in California, biologists have determined the minimum seasonal flows necessary to sustain the salmon runs. And on the Missouri, scientists have constructed a hydrographic model that shows the range of seasonal flows necessary to sustain spawning by the endangered pallid sturgeon and nesting by the piping plover.

Who should make the determination is best answered by reference to the federal-state structure of the Clean Water Act, under which the Environmental Protection Agency sets overall standards and methodologies, giving the states the option to administer the program. States also need incentives to adopt and enforce river-protection plans, and those incentives should ideally be a mix of some carrots—federal grants to aid in implementation—and a stick—withholding federal water development funds from states that do not comply. If the federal government is going to continue, as it surely will, in its historic role of promoting water development through flood-control projects, water and sewer infrastructure grants, and myriad other programs that encourage and promote development and water consumption, those programs should at least require minimal protection of what is left of our lakes, rivers, and landscape ecosystems.

The notion of linking federal development assistance with comprehensive environmental protections for water resources, while not a common practice, is not entirely without precedent. In 1978, upon becoming governor of Arizona, I began making annual trips to Washington to testify in favor of water projects for my state. The subject of my pleas for assistance was the Central Arizona Project, then among the largest and most expensive undertaking in the entire history of federal water projects, a project designed to bring water across the deserts from the Colorado River to Phoenix and Tucson.

In the course of making my case to Congress and the Carter administration, I was reminded that the 1968 legislation authorizing the project included a provision that prohibited the delivery of Central Arizona Project water to any areas of the state that did not have an adequate regulatory program to control groundwater depletion. For years Phoenix and Tucson and the agricultural regions between those cities had been pumping groundwater far beyond the natural recharge rate, a practice that would eventually exhaust the resource, leaving the region with an uncertain future.

As project construction moved forward year by year, the mandate to Arizona to manage its aquifers was ignored, until eventually a new secretary of the interior, Cecil Andrus, began to inquire of the governor what the state intended to do to comply with the law. To which I gave the time-honored western response, in essence, "it's none of your business. Send the money, stay in Washington, and we'll do as we please with our water."

That was in public. In private I began talking with the secretary. I acknowledged that the time to act was at hand, both because the law required it and because to do so would be in Arizona's best interest. But, I cautioned, we would have to play our public roles as adversaries in order to provide me the necessary political cover. He agreed and soon issued a statement that if Arizona did not act, he would consider killing the project by withdrawing administration support for further funding.

That got our attention. I responded by denouncing federal interference and waving the flag of states' rights. Aided by a fortuitous state court decision that cast a cloud of uncertainty over existing water uses, I then gathered the leaders of Arizona's water establishment—municipal water providers, irrigation district leaders, representatives of the mining industry, and key legislators—behind closed doors and suggested that we needed to set aside the rhetoric and get down to the business of drafting a state groundwater-management law. We met weekly for nearly eight months in lengthy, intense bargaining sessions, from which a consensus gradually emerged. At one crucial point, as the effort seemed to falter, I again called the secretary, reviewed the problem, and suggested that it was time for another public threat—which he promptly issued and to which I immediately objected.

By June 1980 we had negotiated and drafted a two-hundred-page groundwater code. I called a special session of the legislature, and within a week it enacted the legislation as submitted without adding or deleting a single word, for fear of upsetting a very delicate set of compromises.

This Central Arizona Project episode clearly demonstrates how effective environmental management can and should be combined with federal assistance, and the threat of withholding that assistance. This should become a routine feature of federal development programs. The annual budget of the Army Corps of Engineers has reached more than eight billion dollars, most of it devoted to dredging and building locks, reservoirs, and flood control projects in every state and congressional district in the country. These projects are a perfect platform for implementing a system of incentives: Corps spending in a given state could be conditioned on the adoption of a comprehensive program of river protection for the entire watershed in which the development assistance is being spent.

IT IS NOT SUFFICIENT just to save the remaining fragments of our natural river systems, however. Just as we have awakened to the possibilities for restoring the land, we should now take steps to bring our dead and dying rivers back to life. A good place to begin is at the dams, where development and land use decisions are set in motion by allocation and use of the water stored behind these structures. Most of the dams built in the twentieth century were planned and constructed by two federal agencies, the Army Corps of Engineers and the Bureau of Reclamation. And, as with the interstate highway system and other federal infrastructure initiatives, little or no planning attention was paid to the land use consequences of dam building.

There are by most estimates more than seventy-five thousand dams blocking our rivers, which amounts to one dam erected each day since Thomas Jefferson took office as president. Nearly every river in the contiguous forty-eight states has been dammed. The Yellowstone River, which runs from within the national park to its confluence with the Missouri, is the longest of the few rivers that remain unimpeded. Some of these seventy-five thousand structures are essential to our modern economy, but a large number are now obsolete, and many should never have been built in the first place.

I was not instinctively drawn to the idea of dam removal; I grew up thinking of dams as there forever, as eternal as the pyramids of Egypt. In the Southwest, Hoover Dam was an American icon, an unforgettable sight, its glistening white ramparts transforming the muddy river in the depths of Black Canyon into light and power and progress.

Like many others I was introduced to the notion of dam removal by a book, *The Monkey Wrench Gang*, Edward Abbey's novel in which a picaresque band of saboteurs scheme to take down the Glen

Canyon Dam, located on the Colorado River just upstream from the Grand Canyon. And I happened to be at that dam, accompanying Secretary of the Interior James Watt, on the day in 1981 when Earth First! pranksters unfurled a huge poster crack down the face of the dam. It was great theater, prompted by an entertaining novel, but removing Glen Canyon Dam seemed far-fetched given its central role in capturing and storing the highly variable annual flows of a river that supplies water to Phoenix, Las Vegas, and Los Angeles.

I awakened to the real-world possibilities of dam removal in the Pacific Northwest, a region that I came to know well only after becoming secretary of the interior. In 1993 I visited Olympic National Park, a place of towering forests and snow-capped peaks drained by white-water streams, one of which, the Elwha River, flows into the Strait of Juan de Fuca at the town of Port Angeles. Salmon, including chinook, coho, sockeye, pink, and chum, as well as steelhead, once spawned in the Elwha and its tributary streams. These runs disappeared in 1910 with the construction of two dams a few miles upstream from the mouth of the river, built to generate hydropower for Port Angeles.

The ecological price paid for the two dams included more than fish, for spawning salmon had once sustained eagles, bears, and other natural fishers in addition to feeding the spiritual and physical needs of the Lower Elwha Klallam Tribe living near the river's mouth. From every perspective this seemed an ideal place to initiate a new era of dam removal, and indeed Congress had authorized a study of the impacts of potential dam removal there even before we came into office.

In the summer of 1994 while visiting Yellowstone I dropped in on the annual meeting of Trout Unlimited, an organization of fly-fishers. It seemed like a perfect place to launch a public discussion of the relation between dam building and the decline of salmon throughout the Pacific Northwest. After a brief review of the Elwha

River issues, I turned to the subject of the Columbia River, where the stakes were considerably higher than a few kilowatts of electricity for a small town on the boundary of a national park.

The Columbia is the Mississippi of the West, beginning in the Canadian Rockies, turning south through eastern Washington, and then flowing along the Washington-Oregon border to the Pacific. As Lewis and Clark made their way downriver, they came upon a natural phenomenon as awesome as the herds of buffalo they had passed through on the Great Plains, this one consisting of fish—more than sixteen million salmon swarming as much as a thousand miles upriver each spring and summer, all the way into the remote streams of the Rocky Mountains.

Ever since that time visitors have come to marvel at the poetry and mystery of the salmon runs, wondering just how it is that a fish, after growing to maturity in the depths of the Pacific, can unerringly find its way upstream for hundreds of miles to spawn in the very tributary where it began life several years earlier. Scientists inform us that the salmon navigates primarily by a sense of smell—what scientists call "olfactory imprinting"—so discriminating that it can discern the equivalent of a single drop of vermouth in a million barrels of gin. The homing process remains mysterious, but it leads again out onto the land. Rainfall is pure distilled water. Falling on the land it begins to dissolve minerals, plant matter, and whatever else may be present, imparting to each tributary a distinctive chemical signature with the power to guide the fish home—and the power to destroy that cycle of life if there is too much sediment or pesticides or PCBs or other contaminants in the flow. The spawning salmon imprints not on the water, but on the land that is dissolved in the water at its birthplace.

Then the Columbia was put to work producing hydropower. The four dams built on the lower river along the Washington-Oregan border—Bonneville, The Dalles, John Day, and McNary—

all incorporated newly designed fish ladders, and the salmon seemed to manage well enough on their downstream voyage to the Pacific and then on the return trip up over the dams and through the reservoirs to spawn in the mountains of Idaho. In 1942 the biggest dam of all, Grand Coulee, was completed at a site in central Washington below the Canadian border; too large for fish ladders, it completely eliminated the salmon runs from thousands of miles of Canadian tributaries.

That left one pathway into the Intermountain West still open: up the Columbia over the four dams and then into the Snake River and on to the Salmon River of central Idaho. And what happened next illustrates two recurring themes in our long history of misusing natural resources. The first is overkill. Dam building that began as reasonable and necessary went on and on beyond all logic, gathering unstoppable political momentum, overstating benefits and underestimating costs, and ignoring environmental impacts. And second, just as occurred in Chesapeake Bay, an ecosystem initially resilient and resistant to stress, eventually reached a cumulative stress threshold and suddenly began to collapse.

The precipitating factor, pushing the river ecosystem to collapse, was a decision by the Army Corps of Engineers to remake the lower Snake River into a shipping channel, for the purpose of extending barge traffic all the way through eastern Washington to the Idaho border. Transforming Lewiston, Idaho, into a seaport was a maniacal idea, an example of the relentless overextension that has characterized many Corps projects. To get barges four hundred miles upriver required transforming the lower Snake into a chain of slackwater lakes impounded behind four more dams, the ostensible purpose of which was to facilitate the shipping of grain and wood pulp to the Port of Vancouver on the lower Columbia. That two transcontinental railroads with sufficient capacity to haul grain already ran parallel to the Columbia did not seem to matter.

The rest of the story was well known to my audience of fly-fishers that day in Yellowstone: the sockeye salmon runs that once turned the lakes of central Idaho red and green in spawning frenzy are now extinct. The Snake River runs of chinook salmon are all on the endangered species list. And the Corps, rather than acknowledging the cause, has resorted to taking salmon out of the river to barge them through the dams—wheat and salmon riding on barges, each taken for a ride along with the taxpayers picking up the bill.

When I concluded there by saying I intended to be the first secretary to tear down a large dam, the audience stood up and cheered. Elsewhere the reaction was less enthusiastic. It was an election year, and nervous western Democrats bombarded the White House with angry complaints. I had again crossed the line, and I had not cleared my remarks with anyone in the White House. Yet, as a practical matter, there was no way to do that. Cabinet members (excepting only the "big four" at State, Treasury, Defense, and Justice) conduct their offices at the outer periphery of the presidency, where new ideas usually get lost or scuttled in the White House bureaucracy. Most cabinet secretaries are expected to spend their time "amplifying" the current administration line, not proposing new ideas or programs. A cabinet officer, for all the prestige associated with the title, is more like the local Ford dealer, expected to sell the product as delivered to his showroom floor and not to appear in Detroit offering unsolicited suggestions to improve the product.

Given this reality of modern executive-branch government, one of the few ways to initiate change is to surface ideas directly in public, watch as they are picked up or discarded by the press and the public, and then be prepared to take the consequences when things go wrong. At a White House reception in 1994, the president took me aside and asked, plainly puzzled, "What's all this talk about tearing down dams?" I explained, somewhat feebly, that I had meant to target the Elwha River dams, not large dams on the Columbia-

Snake river system, but I conceded that in my lack of specificity I had left plenty of room for our opponents to characterize my remarks as an opening volley against the four large dams on the Snake River. He cautioned me to speak more carefully in the future, a fairly mild rebuke considering that he had probably never heard of the idea until angry members of Congress began besieging him with calls.

The deeper problem was that I had once again, as with proposals in mining and grazing reform, failed to anticipate the worsening political climate. This time around, the periodic western "sage-brush rebellion" was merging into the even stronger flames of antigovernment sentiment being fanned in the Gingrich revolution. Within a year the leaders of a new Congress would seek to weaken the Clean Water Act, to repeal the Endangered Species Act, and even to establish a commission to consider closing down national parks. We had come to office with high expectations for reform, and I would instead have to be content to leave town, relentlessly traveling the country simply to defend existing programs and laws.

Yet I also realized the problem was not just hostile members of Congress. The idea of tearing down dams was a novel and unfamiliar concept to the public at large. Dams are impressive structures. They generate clean energy. Why tear down a perfectly good dam that impounded a beautiful blue lake? The ecological damage was, in contrast, more subtle and difficult to explain. Dam removal was a new concept that needed more time to incubate; we would have to back off and seek a better time and place to make a more convincing case. With the Republican takeover of Congress after the 1994 elections, though, it was not clear whether that time would ever come.

IN THE SECOND Clinton administration the political climate thawed a bit, just enough to revisit the subject of dam removal. This time, sensitized by my unhappy experience in the Northwest, we broadened the search, seeking a smaller dam on a less controversial river in friendlier surroundings. The search for a fresh start soon led us away from the Pacific Northwest and, unexpectedly, back to the Atlantic coast, where we went back in time to rediscover some remnants of early American history—hundreds of obsolete dams.

In colonial times dams built to power waterwheels were the only source of mechanical power to run the grist- and sawmills. Wherever settlers went, the nearby stream would soon have a waterwheel and a dam that both diverted water and blocked the passage of fish. Then as the Industrial Revolution began, factory owners began to build larger dams on bigger rivers to power the textile mills springing up from Maine to the Carolinas. In the twentieth century, as electric power displaced waterwheels, the small mills that once dotted the landscape were abandoned, and the hundreds of dams that powered them were often left behind and forgotten.

We began looking for restoration opportunities and soon found an ideal target in North Carolina on the Neuse River. As dams go, the Quaker Neck was not much to look at. All of six feet high, more weir than dam, it had been constructed near the mouth of the river in 1952 to create a pool large enough to supply a short canal that diverted water for cooling at a coal-fired power plant just back from the river. If the dam was unimposing, the ecological consequences were not. The Neuse River, running more than one hundred and fifty miles from the foothills of the Appalachians across North Carolina to Pamlico Sound, had once teemed with spawning stripers, shad, and herring. Records suggest that before the dam was built, North Carolina produced more stripers and shad than any other state; and the Neuse generated more than any other river in the state. After the dam went up, fisheries virtually disappeared. To the American shad, striped bass, alewife, herring, and sturgeon trying to spawn upstream, those six feet might as well have been six hundred, blocking off more than nine hundred miles of upstream spawning waters in the Neuse and its tributaries.

Sportsmen groups in North Carolina had begun to see the attractive possibilities of dam removal. A plan was formulated with the help of state officials and the Fish and Wildlife Service. Hydrologists and engineers were employed to figure out an alternative water diversion method, thereby rendering the dam obsolete and open to removal.

On a spring day in 1997, I went down to the dam site to join utility executives, environmentalists, fishers, and local residents for the ceremony. I took a couple of swings with a sledgehammer against the concrete, then stepped back to watch as a crane swung a wrecking ball to demolish the structure.

And, just a year later, the shad returned right on cue, as if they had been waiting right below the dam all this time. They spawned seventy-five miles upstream, all the way to the state capitol, where residents were soon catching stripers and shad within the city limits. With this example under way, communities up and down the Atlantic coast began looking at possibilities for removal of dams and the restoration of fisheries on their rivers.

Fortified by this success we turned to a large dam, the Edwards Dam in Maine. Located in Augusta, near the mouth of the Kennebec River, the dam was a stone and timber structure built in 1837 to power a textile mill. Nathaniel Hawthorne witnessed the dam's construction and took the occasion to lament the destruction of the river fishery.

The Edwards came up for its fifty-year licensing hearing in 1987. An indecisive proceeding before the Federal Energy Regulatory Commission dragged on for years, and our first attempt in 1993 to settle the conflict through mediation failed. After a cooling-off period the Department of the Interior joined with a new mediator and eventually a complex agreement—calling for the purchase and dismantling of the dam and for mitigation of environmental degradation attendant to expansion of the nearby Bath shipworks— broke the impasse and cleared the way for settlement, license revocation, and removal, the first such outcome in the eighty-year history of the commission.

We gathered on a sunny morning in Augusta, arriving early so we could cast off into the river to fish for stripers, and were soon headed into the turbulent waters below the dam. In the water beneath us the striped bass circled, haplessly searching for a way through the dam. An osprey spiraled overhead, then plunged into the waters to seize a fish. On a ledge above the dam we could see the brick skeleton of the long-abandoned textile mill.

We moved up to the ledge to watch as crews at the dam opened a cut and the waters surged through. Within days the fifteen-mile lake behind the dam disappeared. Within a year there were hordes of fish swarming up the river. This dam breaching made the national press, the sure sign that we had come full circle from those discouraging days after my Yellowstone speech. And now I could return to Olympic National Park; after a five-year struggle in congressional appropriation committees, we had finally obtained funds to begin dismantling the two dams on the Elwha River. Dam removal and river restoration were now on the American agenda, with removal projects springing up in local communities throughout the nation.

The events leading to removal of Edwards Dam and the two dams on the Elwha River were triggered by the Federal Water Power Act of 1920, which requires utility companies and other nonfederal owners to obtain a license from the Federal Energy Regulatory Commission — good for no more than fifty years, subject to renewal — to operate hydro power dams. This licensing requirement provides an important opportunity to review dam operation in light of changing conditions, and advancing technology, and to consider new license conditions to mitigate or reduce impacts upon fish and wildlife.

There is, however, no such licensing requirement for dams operated by the Army Corps of Engineers, the Bureau of Reclamation, or other federal agencies. These dams should be subjected to the same periodic assessment and licensing procedures required for nonfederal dams.

Dam removal, better land management to prevent the decline of our fisheries due to water pollution, better water allocation policies to shape and control the sprawling growth of our cities, laws to ensure against excessive diversions that destroy our rivers and lakes—the subjects discussed in this chapter have two common themes, one physical and the other political. The waters that surround us cannot be simply divided up, used and thrown away like commodities from a store shelf. Everyone lives downstream from someone else, and how we use water in one place has repercussions throughout that watershed, for wildlife, for the land, and for our own well-being.

From this physical reality comes a political imperative. Water cannot be the exclusive concern of any one jurisdiction, local, state, or federal. Our waters must be used and managed in a holistic blend of development and ecological protection, engaging government at every level—beginning with national leadership.

5

Land of the Free

IN THE SPRING OF 1998 several Native American leaders urgently requested a meeting with me to voice concerns about threats to a sacred mountain called the San Francisco Peaks. I was familiar with the mountain, an extinct volcano that dominates the skyline above Flagstaff where I was raised. And I had a pretty good idea of its religious significance to the Navajo, the Hopi, and to other tribes living in the region. I was less certain of the exact nature of the threat, except that it involved a mine somewhere on the eastern flank of the mountain. I agreed to a meeting and a visit to the site.

We gathered in Flagstaff in early June. Walking to the meeting place at the Forest Service complex, I gazed at the sacred mountain looming over us, the forested slopes sweeping upward to the multiple summits, sparkling in the morning air, six thousand feet above the town. What were they mining, I wondered, that could possibly justify intruding into this place?

Ferrell Sekakaku, a traditional leader from the Snake Clan, began the meeting by locating the mountain at the center of Hopi cosmology. On the summits reside the kachinas, spirit figures who mediate between the forces of the cosmos above and the people below living in their pueblos out on the mesas. In winter the kachinas descend from the mountain and enter the Hopi pueblos, taking up residence in the underground kivas, emerging periodically for ceremonials that extend into midsummer. Then, in mid-July the kachinas gather in the plazas for the climatic ceremony, the Niman Kachina, preparatory to returning to the mountain heights.

As he spoke my thoughts drifted back to distant childhood summers when my parents had taken us out to the pueblos to witness the Niman Kachina. I could still feel the heat of the midday sun and hear the mesmerizing chant of the masked figures gathered in the plaza. With the onset of evening, the shadows lengthened and the kachina figures filed through the narrow passages and out to the edge of the mesa where they paused in the fading light, silhouetted against the sky. Then they stepped off the edge, disappearing from sight, traveling through space and time toward the heights of the sacred mountain a hundred miles away, but clearly visible, seeming to float on the horizon in the last light of the setting sun. It was an unforgettable moment, as beautiful and transcendent and true as any religious experience.

The meeting concluded, we drove north on Highway 89 and turned onto a dirt track leading toward the inner basin of the mountain. Leaving the vehicles, we hiked through a fragrant forest of ancient ponderosa pines. Sekakaku continued to talk of Hopi tradition, of the difficulties of bringing up a new generation attentive to the old ways, and of his own experience in a Bureau of Indian Affairs boarding school where students were forbidden to speak Hopi and were admonished by a sign at the entrance that "tradition is the enemy of progress."

We crested a rise and came to the edge of a large open pit that was the White Vulcan Mine. From here we could see the power shovels and drag lines and trucks on the floor of the pit, and at the far end the piles of mined material. A mine representative arrived to explain the operation. The mined material was pumice, a form of consolidated volcanic ash laid down in an ancient eruptive phase of the volcano. Pumice, he explained, is used in the manufacture of building blocks, somewhat like sand but yielding a stronger, more resilient product. Its most profitable market, though, was the garment industry, which uses the material to stone-wash designer jeans to give that faded, preworn fashion look. An elderly Navajo looked down at his worn Levis, rubbed his palm across his leg and commented, "The best way to get a pair of faded jeans is by working in them."

We then heard from the mine representative: "The White Vulcan Mine is not violating any law. It has the legal right to be here. The Mining Law gives us an absolute right to stake a claim anywhere on public land. And if you look around, you can see this is a small mine. There is plenty of space left for the Indians to worship their gods."

I turned to hear from the Navajos, who were eager to tell their story and make it known that this mountain was not exclusively for Hopi kachinas. Wondering if this was about to become a repeat of Christian sects feuding over holy sites in Jerusalem, I listened. In Navajo tradition the mountain is also sacred, one of four marking the boundaries of their ancient homeland. From these heights the Holy People, the mythological forebears of the Navajo, descended into this world to create the people, the Dine, and the plants and animals to sustain them. In this story was no hint of exclusivity, just sacred ground not to be disturbed.

Traditional Navajo medicine men still make pilgrimages to the mountain to gather plants and minerals for ceremonial uses. An apprentice medicine man learning to perform the Blessingway Ceremony, a complex nine-day ritual prayer for harmony and well-being, must prepare by ascending the mountain to first water where he takes a ritual bath, drying himself with cornmeal and dressing in ceremonial buckskin. Continuing up the mountainside he gathers a handful of the sacred earth to place in his medicine bundle. Then to appease the spirit of the mountain he carefully smoothes the surface and scatters a few chips of turquoise. Glancing again at the pits gouged out of the valley below, I wondered if there was enough turquoise in all of the Southwest to appease the spirit of the mountain for this mine.

White Vulcan—where did that name come from? No one seemed to know, but it surely referred to the Roman god of fire, an apt name for a mine on a volcano. The name San Francisco Peaks was no mystery; Franciscan missionaries reaching the Hopi villages in the sixteenth century had named it after Saint Francis, intending both to honor the founder of their order and to discourage the kachina cult that emanated from the mountain.

The Hopis, however, persisted in the old ways, refusing to relinquish the home of the kachinas. Finally, in 1984, they persuaded Congress to designate the mountain summits as the Kachina Peaks Wilderness. But the name San Francisco Peaks remains on the maps. Which god and whose land ethic, I wondered, will finally prevail in the struggle for use and control of this numinous mountain?

We remained at the edge of the pit long enough to make statements for the reporters along on the trip. Then came the inevitable question: did I intend to stop this desecration by shutting down the mine and evicting the operators?

I hesitated. There was little question that White Vulcan had legal precedence over the kachinas. But this was not an isolated incident; conflicts over mining on public lands such as this were popping up all over the West, often due to a new and highly destructive gold-mining process called heap leaching. Heap-leach miners get at low-grade ore by removing entire mountains, crushing the rock, drenching it in cyanide solution, and leaving a moonscape of open pits, waste-rock dumps and finely crushed tailings, and polluted water.

If the facts on this mountain were somewhat unusual, they nonetheless illustrated a larger question that needed to be addressed: should public lands be viewed as a commodity, primarily important for extractive economic use, or should they be endowed with a larger purpose, to be maintained as a great public commons, to be accessible, enjoyed, and used primarily for their natural and spiritual values? And in the case of conflicts, which view should prevail? In the short run, all I could offer the Navajos and Hopis was a promise to appoint a mediator and to come back in a year to report on my progress.

PUBLIC LANDS, the lands held and administered by the federal government, constitute nearly a third of the land area of the United States, almost seven hundred million acres in all, a land mass nearly the size of Mexico. About 40 percent of these lands are located in Alaska, the remainder mostly in the western states. These public lands are administered by four separate land management agencies, each with a different, legislatively defined mission. Three of these agencies are relatively well known: the National Park Service, the U.S. Fish and Wildlife Service, and the U.S. Forest Service. The fourth, lesser-known agency, the Bureau of Land Management in the Department of the Interior, administers the remainder.

BLM lands constitute nearly half of the total area of all public lands, about three hundred million acres. BLM lands are scattered in seemingly random patterns throughout the West. Typically they are the lower-elevation lands — arid expanses of piñon and juniper, shortgrass plains, and sage- and cactus-dominated deserts, the great spaces that you encounter driving across Nevada or Utah or through the deserts of California and Arizona. They are the left-overs, what remained in public ownership after settlers and home-steaders passed them over in search of better-watered lands. Today they remain with the BLM, left over again after the higher-elevation forested lands were carved out for national forests and after some of the most scenic areas and regions rich in wildlife were given over for national parks and wildlife refuges.

The exact rationale for continuing public ownership and the preferred uses of this huge plate of leftover lands has never been entirely settled. However, as the western spaces begin to fill in with development (Nevada is the fastest growing state, closely followed by Arizona), the need for planning is becoming ever more apparent. Conflicting demands for minerals, for energy development, and for wildlife and open space underline the need for workable priorities and land use plans.

Remote though they may be, BLM lands have not gone unused. For generations they have largely been the exclusive province of miners and ranchers, both in fact and in law. The California gold rush in 1849 brought prospectors swarming across the West searching for gold and silver. In response to demands for title to their discoveries, Congress enacted the Mining Law of 1872, which provided that miners could take title to a strike by staking a claim and then filing for a deed with the local land office. Ranchers were not far behind, driving herds of cattle and sheep onto the land, and claiming rights by the fact of occupancy. Legal recognition of their presence on the land, however, did not come until 1934 when Congress passed the Taylor Grazing Act, which provided that most public lands would be available for livestock grazing and authorized issuance of grazing permits to ranchers then in possession of the land. With these two laws—the Mining Law of 1872 and the Taylor Grazing Act—miners and ranchers were effectively given priority on public lands, a framework that endures to the present day.

The grazing of livestock is the most damaging use of public land, not least because cattle and sheep are ubiquitous on western lands, grazing from the low deserts on up the mountainsides to where grass gives out at the timberline. Livestock are present in many areas where the land is too fragile for any grazing at all, and almost everywhere there are too many animals for the land to support in a sustainable manner.

Early on, ranchers set out to eliminate any wildlife considered a threat to their livestock. When my grandfather arrived in Arizona in 1886 to start a ranching operation, grizzlies had already been eliminated. Wolves disappeared within a generation. Cougars were next, driven to the edge of survival in remote, inaccessible canyons. Then coyotes and bobcats. Sheepherders laced animal carcasses with strychnine to clear the skies of golden eagles, supposedly a threat to their lambs. Then government agents charged with "predator control" arrived, helping to poison out the remaining colonies of prairie dogs and ferrets. In my generation the rangelands of northern Arizona were silent and lonely places where you could travel for hours without seeing or hearing a wild creature other than an occasional jackrabbit or a sparrow streaking through the junipers.

In recent years the wildlife that survived this rangeland massacre has been making a slow comeback. But the land itself, grievously lacerated, is still sick and hardly recovering. The damage from decades of overgrazing is everywhere apparent, in the denuded banks of streams and washes, stripped of the willow thickets that once held them in place; in desert water holes trampled into muddy bogs; in the expanses of grama grass grazed to the roots, opening the ground to cheatgrass and other exotic invaders.

As western regions developed into the twentieth century, the near absolute priority status accorded ranching and mining did not go unchallenged. As grazing denuded the land and mine wastes poisoned the streams, newcomers were arriving, residents from nearby cities demanding access to the land for hunting and fishing or for just the enjoyment of wildlife, clean waters, and clear horizons. The rise of a recreation and tourism industry with large economic benefits brought a new user lobby into the mix of public-lands policy.

In 1976 Congress attempted to address the resulting conflicts by enacting the Federal Land Policy and Management Act, which established that the remaining public lands would be retained in federal ownership. For what purpose, however, was less clear. The act spelled out procedural requirements for public participation in land use decision making and the periodic preparation and updating of what were called resource management plans. The legislation, however, did not loosen the stranglehold of mining and ranching interests, for it did not repeal either the Mining Law of 1872 or the Taylor Grazing Act.

The best the sponsors could do to address use conflicts was to include language known as "multiple use," suggesting that every interest should have unimpeded access, irrespective of the damage that may be caused to other users or to the land itself. In practice, multiple use has proven to be little more than a new name for the old practice of according mining and grazing preferential access to public lands, with a footnote that the public remains free to hunt, fish, and camp amid the wreckage.

As the Clinton administration came to office in 1993, it seemed that at last the time was ripe for public lands reform. We began with two basic concepts, one to reform grazing practices, the other to revise the mining law. The overall objective of grazing reform would be to reduce livestock numbers to sustainable levels. The mining reform would require payment of royalties and a determination whether mining was an appropriate use of the land after taking into consideration environmental and public-use issues.

Our effort, however, was star-crossed almost from the very beginning. The Office of Management and Budget began by including, with little consultation, a whopping fee increase for grazing permits in the president's budget, so inflaming the opposition that the president's chief of staff backed down by retracting the proposal, which in turn prompted the national press to crow that the new president was incapable of standing up to Congress. Correctly sensing that the president was not going to invest political capital in a fight on this issue, the opposition, thus emboldened, killed grazing reform legislation in a Senate filibuster. Mining reform legislation died in a Senate-House conference committee.

Sorting through the wreckage, we turned to look at laws already on the books to see how we might make better use of the authority we already possessed. And once again we discovered new possibilities in the Endangered Species Act. In the process we learned that the case for restoration did not always have to be packaged as "grazing regulations," a label that seemed to induce drowsiness in even the most attentive members of Congress and the press. This time around, reform would have a new leader, a charismatic actor with the power to capture and hold public attention: *Canis lupus*, the gray wolf.

THE WAR TO ERADICATE the wolf began as soon as ranchers came onto western lands. Over time that war intensified into a savage campaign of trapping, shooting, and poisoning, often led by bounty hunters subsidized by the government. By 1930 the process was complete: the few stragglers had been eliminated and there were no wolves to be found anywhere in the West outside Alaska.

Over the course of the twentieth century public attitudes toward the wolf gradually began to shift as Aldo Leopold, the Muries, and other researchers described the functioning and importance of large predators in healthy ecosystems, and as Americans became more interested in the condition of wildlife on public lands. A movement to restore the wolf got under way in the 1980s; the Fish and Wildlife Service, with the authority conferred by the Endangered Species Act, took up the cause and began working with Canada to find suitable populations for a transplant effort. The livestock industry marshaled its forces in opposition, but succeeded only in slowing the process. What we and they were learning was that the wolf had a national constituency of public support, and members of Congress from outside the West consistently backed the program.

In the winter of 1994, wolves were brought to Yellowstone and to several locations in northern Idaho. Ranchers fought back, in court and in Congress. But the wolf, once back on the land, was unstoppable. Today there are several hundred wolves adding their grace and beauty to wild spaces. Tens of thousands of visitors from all over the country come to Yellowstone to see them, and livestock losses have proven to be minimal; more livestock are killed by lightning than by wolves.

The next step in restoring public lands was to use the Endangered Species Act to control and reduce the overgrazing that has caused so much destruction throughout the West. And the leader in this effort would turn out to be none other than the desert tortoise, whose listing as an endangered species has played such an important role in containing sprawl in Las Vegas, as discussed in chapter 2.

The tortoise is a creature that has survived virtually unchanged since it first appeared in the geologic record more than 150 million years ago. The species became threatened, however, when ranchers began driving their herds onto Mojave Desert lands for spring grazing, at the very time that the tortoise awakens from hibernation and emerges from its burrow to graze on the greening desert shrubs and grasses. As livestock trampled the burrows and monopolized the scarce desert vegetation, tortoise populations plummeted.

To protect tortoise habitat, the Fish and Wildlife Service in 1994 designated more than six million acres of the Mojave as critical habitat. It then issued a management plan sharply limiting spring livestock grazing, and in some especially sensitive areas it terminated grazing altogether.

In 1995 another species with widespread habitat requirements, and therefore even greater potential to change grazing practices, flew onto the endangered species list. The southwestern willow flycatcher is a migratory bird that winters in Costa Rica and other parts of Central America, returning north in the spring to breed and nest in the dense thickets of willow, seep willow, and cottonwood that once crowded small desert streams in Arizona, New Mexico, and parts of Southern California and Nevada. The decline of the fly-catcher is the direct consequence of the destruction of stream courses by livestock, which congregate in the bottoms, watering and grazing and trampling the vegetation down to rock and gravel. The listing of the flycatcher and other riparian-dependent species, including several small desert fish species, prompted Fish and Wildlife to act. Prodded along by litigation, the agency began to require ranchers to adopt riparian protection plans, including fencing to control livestock access, as a condition of retaining their grazing permits.

The steadily increasing number of desert species appearing on the endangered species list sent a message not to be ignored: in this dry and spare desert environment the land simply cannot with-stand the pressure of livestock at any stocking level. Prior to settle-ment, the Mojave and Sonoran deserts of the Southwest had never been subjected to extensive grazing, and the fragile plant cover had thus not evolved to tolerate the activity. The desert is a wondrous, beautiful place; it is also lean and unforgiving. There is no surplus for introduced grazing animals.

These desert lands will not retain their natural diversity, much less undergo natural regeneration, until livestock grazing is removed. Exactly where to draw the geographic line—the exact place where deserts give way to grasslands that can sustain grazing —has not received much study. Eventually, scientific research will give us the information we need to decide where best to draw these lines. Many ecologists believe that the line should be drawn at ten inches of rainfall per year (for comparison Atlanta receives fifty inches, San Francisco twenty-two, and Phoenix eight). That com-ports with my experience, and I conclude that livestock should be removed from public lands where there is less than ten inches of rainfall.

In recent years several conservation organizations have devised a simple and very encouraging approach to the reduction and eventual elimination of desert livestock grazing. These groups offer to buy out grazing permits in voluntary, willing-seller transactions, thus bypassing the contentious political fights over uncompensated regulatory reductions. Although no legally recognized property rights accrue to BLM grazing permits (which are just that, permits) the purchase and retirement of these permits can be a good bargain on both sides. In the desert regions, a rancher typically owns several hundred or a few thousand acres, patched together from old homesteads. Such acreage typically serves as the private "base property" to support grazing leases on tens of thousands of acres of public land. In these regions where it may take a hundred acres or more to feed a single animal, grazing rights can be purchased and retired at market value for small sums relative to the conservation value of the land.

In a recent transaction the Conservation Fund and the Grand Canyon Trust purchased the Kane Ranch north of the Grand Canyon on the Colorado Plateau, consisting of about a thousand acres of private land and grazing rights on nearly a million acres of public land for the appraised value of four and a half million dollars. That pencils out to less than five dollars per acre for protection of some of the most spectacular land in the West, which can now be restored to benefit the famed Kaibab deer herd, free-ranging pronghorn antelope, desert bighorn sheep, and scores of other species.

The logic of preserving desert ecosystems by eliminating livestock grazing does not necessarily extend to phasing out grazing on all public lands. There are many robust forest and grassland systems, with more than ten inches of annual rainfall, that can withstand moderate, properly regulated grazing. And in fact these higher altitude ecosystems, many located within the national forests, have evolved with grazing elk and other large herbivores. In these landscapes cattle and elk are direct competitors for forage, and while more cattle may mean fewer elk, that remains a choice appropriately made after taking into account local preferences.

IN THE GEORGE W. BUSH ADMINISTRATION, the unrestrained push for energy production has also emerged as a serious threat to the public lands. In the rush to throw open lands for drilling, the administration has cast overboard even the most minimal measures for protection of the land, water, and wildlife. The unprecedented effort to open the Arctic National Wildlife Refuge to exploration is only the most outrageous example of a process that is taking place on public lands throughout the nation.

The case for making some public lands available for oil and gas exploration is strong. Leaving aside the egregious failures of the Bush administration to promote conservation and renewable energy, the fact remains that oil and gas will continue to play a significant, if reduced role in our national energy equation for generations to come.

Comparing energy production to traditional livestock grazing provides an instructive contrast in economics and environmental values. Energy production has substantial economic implications for the nation; even though we can never achieve energy independence in oil and gas, domestic production does help with our balance of payments and at least marginally reduces dependence on volatile foreign sources. Livestock grazing, which has caused so much damage to the land, is of minor significance in the national economy. Public lands produce less than 5 percent of the beef consumed in the country; there are more cattle in New York than in Nevada, more in Virginia than in Arizona. While livestock production can easily be moved to the Midwest or other more suitable regions, oil and gas fields cannot be moved to more convenient locations.

The production of oil and gas can also be less damaging to the land than either grazing or mining. Grazing renders vast areas inhospitable for native species, and hard-rock mining typically tears up large surface expanses and generates toxic tailings and waste that find their way into the waters. Oil and gas are subsurface deposits, which can in theory be pumped from underground reservoirs with relatively little surface disturbance.

And unlike livestock grazing and hard-rock mining, which are accorded the statutory preferences set out in the Taylor Grazing Act and the Mining Law of 1872, oil and gas production on public lands is governed by a separate and quite progressive statute, the Mineral Leasing Act of 1920 (which notwithstanding the title applies mainly to the fossil fuels—oil, gas, and coal). This law gives the Bureau of Land Management discretionary authority to lease lands for exploration, drilling, and production. The BLM has discretion not only to withhold sensitive lands from leasing, but also to impose any manner of conditions to minimize negative impacts on lands that it does lease.

These distinctions should make it possible to find common ground in the formulation of oil and gas leasing policy. But that has not occurred, due in no small measure to the propensity of the energy industry to cut corners in ways that are environmentally destructive whenever no one is looking, and often even when they are.

OUR OPPORTUNITY DURING the Clinton years to demonstrate how the Mineral Leasing Act could be used to strike a balance between the dual imperatives of energy production and environmental protection came as a consequence of the controversy over the Arctic National Wildlife Refuge. We began by drawing a line at the Arctic Refuge. Some places have natural values beyond calculation, not to be compromised by drilling. There are, however, extensive public lands with good oil prospects located along the coastal plain that extends west of Prudhoe Bay toward Siberia. Although this region lies outside the refuge, it too has a large caribou herd and the land is dotted with shallow lakes that provide some of the most important waterfowl nesting habitat in the entire Arctic. Nevertheless, some portion of the lands west of Prudhoe Bay seemed the logical place to plan a careful expansion of oil exploration, if we could do so without undue disturbance to the region's ecology. In 1998 we began to formulate a leasing program that would open up the region, subject to three important conditions.

The building of roads is the most destructive aspect of energy production. Roads not only scar the land and disrupt wildlife patterns, they inevitably open the landscape to unrelated traffic and to land speculation. All over the globe, wherever oil exploration and development is preceded by road construction, it opens entire regions to unrestrained invasion, random development, and all too often, the destruction of indigenous cultures. In the Amazon, the Congo Basin, Sumatra, and elsewhere, it is not the extraction of oil and gas per se, but the unnecessary disruption of wildlife, forest habitat, and indigenous communities that evokes so much opposition to oil exploration.

Road building is no longer necessary for oil development, except in limited circumstances. With the advent of helicopter transport, there is no need to open the Arctic to further disruption by road building, and accordingly we imposed as our first leasing condition that no bridges could be built across the Colville River and no roads beyond into the western Arctic plain.

The second condition was to place especially sensitive regions off-limits to drilling. In this case that meant the area around Teshekpuk Lake, where molting geese, unable to fly as they grow new feathers, are especially sensitive to disturbance.

The third condition required use of advanced technology,

including the use of slant drilling, a technique that enables the drilling of multiple wells extending outward for several miles from a single drilling pad. This technique, long-used on ocean drilling platforms, substantially reduces the footprint of oil- and gas-production facilities.

With these conditions we moved toward a new model for oil leasing, one that would allow drilling within a quasi wilderness that could revert to the wildlife commons once the companies had extracted their last barrel of oil, closed down, and left. While these stipulations would increase the expense of bringing oil into production, given the prospects for continually increasing energy prices, the companies voiced only mild objections, and in 2000 the leasing program began with an offering of more than four million acres.

Then in 2004 the Bush administration announced that leasing in the western Arctic would be accelerated and the protective conditions dropped. The region west of the Colville River would be open to road building, and Teshekpuk Lake would be open for drilling not only along the shoreline, but in the waters of the lake as well. As if to underline its contempt for the environmental safeguards, it even cut back the boundaries of a goose-molting preserve that had been originally established in the 1980s by a notoriously industry-friendly secretary, James Watt.

A disquieting preview of what may be in store for the Alaska Refuge can be seen in the upper Green River valley of Wyoming. There, on BLM lands known as the Jonah Field, some five hundred producing gas wells are located on about fifty square miles of high desert habitat favored by the rare sage grouse and declining herds of pronghorn antelope. In February 2005 the BLM released an environmental impact statement for the Jonah Field, proposing to permit an additional 3,100 new wells. This would allow a drilling site on every ten acres, increasing the area of surface disturbance from construction of roads and drilling pads to as much as 34 percent of the total surface area, thus reducing remaining habitat to tattered fragments of little or no value to wildlife.

Suggestions that directional drilling might be required were dismissed as impractical. Meanwhile in California, where state officials take regulation more seriously, the THUMS oil company has used directional drilling to put down over twelve hundred wells from just four drilling pads located in Long Beach Harbor. Suggestions that the spaghetti tangles of roads crisscrossing the Green River valley could be reduced by using helicopters are also dismissed, as if to say, "they did that for awhile in Alaska just for some good publicity during the ANWR debate."

Environmental problems related to energy production also exist in the adjoining state of Montana. The BLM is leasing lands for the production of coalbed methane, natural gas stored in subsurface coal beds that extend throughout the region. The gas, confined within the coal beds by natural water pressure, is produced by pumping large volumes of water to the surface to reduce pressure and release the gas. And drillers are dumping the often highly saline water—loaded with sulfates and minerals dissolved from the coal— into nearby streams and ponds and onto the land, threatening to poison fisheries and farmers' crops. Responding to this threat, the BLM under the Bush administration has refused to implement the obvious solution—requiring drillers, once the gas is produced, to reinject the water back into the coal seams from which it was pumped. This administration has the power, yet lacks the will, to produce oil and gas in an environmentally responsible manner.

APART FROM MANAGING resource extraction, the large remaining task for the next generation of public-lands students, legislators, and managers is to arrive at a stable configuration of lands that should remain permanently in public ownership for the use and enjoyment of generations to come. That question has already mostly been answered for the national parks, wildlife refuges, and national forests, all of which are enclosed within boundaries defined in the laws and executive orders that created them. Such is not the case, however, for remnant lands administered by the BLM, which are still scattered helter-skelter across the West, complicating the planning and management of public and private lands alike.

One look at a land tenure map of the West, or even of a single state, reveals the problem. Public lands are sprinkled across the map in fragments near and far, large and small, regular and irregular. There are large blocks in Nevada, western Arizona, and eastern Oregon, and thousands of small tracts of 40, 80, and 160 acres within western cities and lost inside Indian reservations. A huge checkerboard forty miles wide, the legacy of an early railroad land grant, extends across southern Wyoming. Public lands include much of the Arctic plain of Alaska, thousands of tiny offshore rocks and islands, and an old lighthouse on the Oregon coast.

However interesting the history behind the patterns of these leftovers, accidents of history are hardly a rationale for the retention of lands in public ownership. What, one may ask, is the national interest in continuing to own a hundred acres surrounded by subdivisions in the middle of Tucson? Or of hanging onto the red squares on the checkerboard while the black squares in private ownership are being cut up and sold off in forty-acre "ranchettes" rendering the public half of the checkerboard unfit for wildlife habitat? Or holding onto a few hundred acres isolated in thousands of acres of privately owned ranchland? All these factors strongly suggest the need for a policy that identifies which lands should be retained and how the patterns of public ownership should be arranged and consolidated to serve specified public purposes, primarily the protection of intact ecosystems, watersheds, open space, and wildlife.

The Federal Land Policy and Management Act of 1976, while laudably setting forth a statutory presumption that public lands should be retained in public ownership, did not provide much guidance for the consolidation of those lands into coherent blocks with boundaries similar to national parks and forests, although it did provide authority to exchange lands. In the years since the law's enactment, the BLM has moved cautiously with small-scale consolidation, typically selling or exchanging lands only at the request of public officials or exchanging private holdings isolated within large tracts of public land. These exchange policies have by and large proved beneficial to the cause of conservation. Consolidating public landholdings in the backcountry in exchange for close-in urban lands ripe for development is a smart growth policy. In one celebrated exchange, the BLM acquired an old Mexican land grant extending for thirty miles along both sides of the San Pedro River in southern Arizona—perhaps the most important migratory bird sanctuary in the desert Southwest—in exchange for public lands within the developing margins of greater Phoenix. In the Northwest enlightened BLM managers have been able to build, through many small exchanges, a public corridor along the Deschutes River in western Oregon, one of the renowned steelhead fisheries in the region.

Yet these and many other such examples are only a small start, a process of nibbling at the edges of a very large consolidation effort that should ultimately be undertaken by Congress. Eventually legislation would be desirable for designating a system of permanent national-interest lands, building upon and fleshing out the core areas of current landholdings by means of land exchanges that operate both to dispose of unneeded outlying lands and to acquire important inholdings. A process of land retention on this scale must have structured participation by the states and local governments together with extensive public involvement, for it will mean decisions of great consequence.

Throughout the modern history of public lands, our presidents have typically taken the lead in making policy. Theodore Roosevelt and several of his predecessors created our system of national forests by designating lands under authority granted by Congress.

In 1906, Congress responded to public concern over the looting of archaeological treasures from Mesa Verde and other newly discovered prehistoric ruins on public lands in the Southwest by passing the Antiquities Act, granting the president authority to set aside and reserve lands, important for their archaeological value, as national monuments.

The antiquities legislation also contained a phrase giving the president power to protect not only ruins, but also and more generally "objects of historic or scientific interest." Serving up that language to Theodore Roosevelt was like offering a sardine to a cat, and he put it to test by proclaiming Grand Canyon National Monument, comprising some 270,000 acres, an area nearly a thousand times larger than anything previously withdrawn for the protection of Indian ruins. When the inevitable lawsuit challenging his authority to set aside such a large expanse reached the Supreme Court in 1920, the justices unanimously upheld the president's action, reasoning simply that while Congress had complete authority over public lands, it was free to delegate management decisions to the president.

Since that time most presidents have followed Roosevelt's lead, and in the twentieth century the Antiquities Act became the primary vehicle for presidential leadership in expanding our national park system. Executive branch proclamations included monument designation for Glacier Bay, Death Valley, and Zion, all of which, like the Grand Canyon, were eventually elevated by Congress to the status of national parks. With these precedents, it was no surprise that President Clinton would make use of the Antiquities Act, but this time it was for something new—creating a system of conservation lands that would be administered by the BLM.

USE OF THE ANTIQUITIES ACT as a land use planning tool has not been without controversy. The act gives the president the power to protect monument lands by withdrawing them from operation of the Mining Law of 1872, the Taylor Grazing Act, and other laws granting priority to extractive uses, which is why mining, ranching, and logging interests consistently oppose monument designations. Western members of Congress have a long history of opposing presidential use of the Antiquities Act for conservation purposes, and they have on occasion managed to retaliate by restricting future application of the law in their state. When after much controversy Franklin Roosevelt created the Jackson Hole National Monument in 1940, Congress eventually responded by exempting Wyoming from further application of the act; and in 1980, in the course of a struggle over Alaska lands, Congress effectively exempted that state too from future proclamations.

Given this regrettable but predictable western hostility, a president often waits until he is a lame duck, about to leave office and thus beyond the reach of congressional backlash, to use the law. President Clinton would prove to be no exception—with one exception. In 1996 he was concluding his first term, campaigning for re-election, and was by no means a lame duck, when Dick Morris, his shadowy, backstage political consultant, ran a poll that showed a surge of interest in environmental issues. Morris, who had no discernable outdoor experience beyond a well-publicized tryst on the balcony of the Jefferson Hotel, nonetheless came up with a big idea—the president should stage a September surprise with a dramatic environmental initiative.

Soon the search was on for an appropriate subject, and before long southern Utah came into focus. The panoramic landscapes of the region had long been of interest to conservationists, going back to a New Deal proposal to set the area aside as a national park. And now there were plans to mine coal deposits beneath the Kaiparowits Plateau, to accelerate drilling for oil and gas, and even to locate a giant complex of coal-fired power plants in the area.

Establishing the Grand Staircase–Escalante National Monument, as it came to be known, was an irresistible idea. Generations of geologists had established the uniqueness of the region, which displays a remarkable stair-step time sequence extending from the primordial depths of the Grand Canyon forward and northward through time to the younger strata of Zion and Bryce Canyon national parks. The president had clear authority under the Antiquities Act to designate a monument, and doing so did not require advance public discussion that would stir controversy and dilute the impact of a surprise announcement. The political repercussions would come later, not something to fret about in the midst of an election campaign.

After a chaotic internal debate and considerable conflict, President Clinton appeared at the south rim of the Grand Canyon on September 26, 1996, to proclaim the Grand Staircase–Escalante National Monument. The proclamation had exactly the effect that Morris predicted—a blaze of favorable publicity in the national press, topped off by television pictures of the president on the rim of the Grand Canyon (located not in Utah but in Arizona, a site less likely to draw demonstrators from southern Utah).

While the Grand Staircase–Escalante decision proved popular in the nation at large, it was less well received in southern Utah, where effigies of the president and his cabinet secretary dangled from lampposts in the streets of Escalante. The state of Utah promptly filed suit to overturn the proclamation and members of the Utah congressional delegation were soon drafting bills to weaken the Antiquities Act. While the bills ultimately failed to move, the controversy did put an end to any further monument discussions within White House circles. By 1998, with the winds of impeachment gathering in Congress, the president needed all the allies he could find, and public-lands initiatives fell by the wayside.

Then in late 1998 another opportunity appeared. The final congressional election of our last term in office was over, and now the president really was a lame duck. There would be one more chance to use the Antiquities Act despite lingering congressional resentment from the Utah experience.

One possibility would be to wait until the last minute, contenting ourselves in the meantime with drawing up a list of opportunities for Clinton to consider during his final week in office. Lyndon Johnson had done that, so had Dwight Eisenhower and even Herbert Hoover. But given the hostility of the Republican Congress to environmental initiatives, it seemed to me entirely possible that the backlash over a list of midnight designations might well carry over into the next Congress, leading to repeal or to a crippling modification of the Antiquities Act. To create more monuments at the price of losing the act itself would hardly constitute progress.

I thought back to Dick Morris. He had correctly gauged public opinion; the Grand Staircase–Escalante proclamation had turned out to be popular not only in the nation at large, but even in much of Utah, where a slight majority had responded favorably in opinion polls taken after the fact. The political problem, then, was not so much the idea of a monument, but the way we had cloaked the process in secrecy right up to the announcement. So why not turn the process on its head—advance monument proposals in public and hold public hearings, spiking complaints of secrecy and using public support to blunt the opposition in Congress?

THE QUESTION WAS where to begin and how to explain and characterize new monument proposals. Looking over the long list of monument proclamations from the past century, it appeared to me that most presidents had selected places that were on the way to becoming national parks, places that exhibited what used to be called "natural curiosities," whether hot springs, waterfalls, giant volcanoes, dinosaur bones, petrified wood, gargantuan sequoia trees, natural bridges, or the like.

By the late 1990s, however, it was time for the president's much-traveled rhetorical "bridge to the twenty-first century" to lead not just to another natural bridge or two somewhere out West. Biology coupled with ecosystem science had become, and is, the dominant paradigm for both understanding public lands and formulating prescriptions for their use and enjoyment. During the century of its existence the Antiquities Act had been interpreted and expanded in response to changing conditions and public expectations. It began with concerns over vandalism of archaeological sites and expanded to preserving geological phenomena and, under President Carter, to protecting entire large landscapes in Alaska. Now we had another opportunity to interpret the phrase "objects of historic or scientific interest" to encompass the concerns of our times — preserving open space threatened by development and saving biodiversity by protecting complete ecosystems.

To set the stage for expanding the reach of the Antiquities Act, we first had to reconsider the role of the Park Service. From the very beginning, establishing national monuments had usually meant transferring the land from the Bureau of Land Management to the Park Service. But as we finished drafting the Grand Staircase–Escalante monument proclamation, I voiced my reservations about the practice. It was time, I thought, to recognize that we were protecting landscapes, not making parks. And that it would be crucially important to encourage the BLM to develop a conservation mission — something unlikely to occur if every new monument carved out of existing public lands were taken away from the BLM and given to the Park Service.

Next we had to consider lingering congressional hostility from the Grand Staircase–Escalante designation. That episode suggested that we needed to select a site with widespread public appeal and that we make the process transparent by inviting public participation. And it suggested we select a state where I had confidence we could manage the predictable hostile response from the congressional delegation. All of these concerns brought us back once again to Arizona and Grand Canyon.

The Grand Canyon was of course already a national park. But the boundaries set by Theodore Roosevelt, generous for their time and subsequently enlarged by presidential and congressional action, were still in need of further expansion. For the most part the park boundaries had been drawn from the perspective of artists, photographers, and other visitors to the familiar vantage points on the south rim. Many parts of the canyon that lay outside and beyond the picture frame were not included. With our vision enhanced and extended by modern hydrology, we could now see beyond the picture frame to include tributaries reaching far into the highlands beyond the north rim. To protect the scenic heart of the canyon, we had to reach out and include these tributary arteries.

Shortly after Thanksgiving of 1998 we organized a camping trip into the Uinkaret Plateau, a remote region immediately north of the western Grand Canyon. We invited several members of the Arizona press, the superintendent of Grand Canyon National Park, and the land managers from the surrounding public lands. Around a campfire beneath the pines, we discussed expanding the protected lands of the Grand Canyon by a third, including the side canyons and drainages that extended from the forests surrounding our campfire.

I recommended that the new monument remain under BLM jurisdiction, citing the same reasons as I had back in my office when we were drawing the boundaries for Grand Staircase–Escalante. Notably, these monuments were not intended to be national parks with highly developed visitor facilities. The purpose of these new monuments was to assert, unequivocally, the primacy of public values on these landscapes, precluding uses that would impair the natural values of the land. But we would not automatically exclude traditional uses such as hunting and grazing, so long as they were managed consistently with the overriding purpose of preserving and restoring the natural systems.

The next morning as we hiked to the summit of Mount Dellenbaugh, someone asked whether this concept of ecosystem-scale monuments should eventually be extended to encompass all significant portions of public lands, at least all those outside established mining areas. It was a provocative question, one that we had not directly confronted. In expanding the reach of the Antiquities Act, we had been scrupulously careful to document the distinctive ecological and scientific characteristics that qualified a given area as an "object of historic or scientific interest." But that phrase is an expansive vessel, whose content has changed considerably in the past and, as noted, presumably could expand still more in the future as perceptions and expectations for public lands continue to evolve. Successive presidents have demonstrated their power, both expansive and flexible, under the Antiquities Act to move up to the next step, from Indian ruins, to "natural curiosities," to proto–national parks, to entire landscapes and ecosystems. And if Congress does not act to clear away the underbrush of outdated special-interest laws and move toward establishing public priorities, perhaps future presidents will continue to extend the process of public lands reform by executive action.

From Mount Dellenbaugh, we looked across the Grand Canyon where, far to the south, I could see the summits of the San Francisco Peaks. Should this sacred mountain be protected as a national monument? The negotiator I had charged with resolving the mining issue on that mountain was nearing a settlement, in which the White Vulcan Mine would shut down, yield its claims, and clean up the remnants in exchange for a payment of one million dollars. There would probably not be time to do more.

We returned from the Uinkaret Plateau to read favorable articles about our trip in the Arizona press, and follow-up stories reported that 70 percent of Arizonans, urban and rural, favored expanded protection for the Grand Canyon in the form of a new national monument. A congressional hearing called to head off the proposal dwindled into incoherence as members began to comprehend the widespread public support.

I had discussed the Grand Canyon proposal briefly with the president before embarking on our camping trip. He was noncommittal, neither enthusiastic nor negative. Of more concern, the political chill from the Grand Staircase–Escalante episode lingered among White House staff, through whom I would have to channel new monument proposals.

So I tried another approach. On one side of an index card I tallied up the land conservation achievements of the Clinton administration, already considerable because of lands protected by the California Desert Protection Act, the Northwest Forest Plan, the habitat conservation plans in Southern California, land acquisitions in Alaska, and the Grand Staircase–Escalante monument designation. In another column, I did a comparative tally for Theodore Roosevelt, adding up his national forests, wildlife refuges, and nineteen national monuments. It was clear that we were competitive—still a considerable ways behind, but within striking distance of what our greatest conservation president had accomplished.

In the reception line at a state dinner for the prime minister of Japan, I greeted President Clinton and handed him the card. He began to stuff it in his jacket pocket, hesitated, looked again, and then as the reception line slowed to a halt he scrutinized the numbers, and then nodded enthusiastically. I moved on, confident that at last we had a mandate to act not just on the Grand Canyon lands but elsewhere. It all came down to one word: legacy.

As time ran out on our second term, we crisscrossed the West. We organized exploratory trips to proposed sites and then returned to nearby communities to hold public discussions, meeting with newspaper editors, parlaying with county commissioners and tribal governments—all the familiar aspects of any political campaign.

As the president evidenced his intention to act on my recommendations and with public opinion behind him, several members of Congress began coming forward to assist with our proposals in their districts. With their support, our recommendations to the president prompted congressional action and legislation establishing the Otay Mountain Wilderness near San Diego, San Jacinto Mountains National Monument above Palm Springs, Las Cienegas National Conservation Area in Arizona, Colorado National Monument and Great Sand Dunes National Park and Preserve in Colorado, and the million-acre Steens Mountain Cooperative Management Area in the high deserts of southeastern Oregon.

Of all the monuments established on our watch, one in Colorado perhaps best illustrates the conceptual transition that underlay our efforts. Ironically the area was not only an "object of historic or scientific interest," it was also an archaeological site squarely within the explicit language of the Antiquities Act. In 1923 President Harding had established Hovenweep National Monument in the Four Corners region of southern Colorado and Utah. The monument originally consisted of six ruins covering only 785 acres, each located tens of miles from the other.

In the intervening century, archaeologists have expanded their vision, moving beyond digging up pottery and other museum pieces to investigating how ancient cultures actually lived in the context of their surroundings. And what they soon discovered was not six isolated ruins but an entire archaeological landscape on which the ancient-pueblo residents hunted, farmed, and established shrines and trading routes, leaving evidence of their presence on nearly every square acre—a kind of archaeological ecosystem. In 2000 the president established Canyons of the Ancients National

Monument, encompassing some of the Hovenweep sites and preserving 164,000 acres, thus expanding the original proclamation
by more than two hundred times.

WHILE ON ONE OF THOSE exploratory trips during this period, I
happened to read *Undaunted Courage*, the best-selling account of
Lewis and Clark and their great voyage of discovery. In the course of
telling the story, author Stephen Ambrose sets a memorable scene
as the cocaptains work their pirogues through the Missouri Breaks,
a river stretch bordered by a fantasy land of white cliffs. At that point
Ambrose steps outside the story, adding a footnote commenting:
"Of all the historic and/or scenic sights we have visited in the world,
this is number one. We have made the trip ten times."

Intriguing. I ordered up the maps and learned that much of the
Missouri Breaks region was shaded in yellow, the symbol for public
lands. There were enough public lands along the river to form the
core of a significant protected area, I realized, notwithstanding the
intermixture of private lands derived from old livestock homesteads scattered along and away from the river.

I placed a call to Ambrose, introduced myself, and we had a
lengthy discussion. He was so enthusiastic that I suggested we take
a trip together through the Breaks. The following summer we
canoed down the river, drifting beneath canopies of cottonwood
and willow at the base of white cliffs as golden eagles circled overhead. As Ambrose read aloud from the journals, I looked about,
thinking how little seemed to have changed in the two hundred
years since Lewis wrote those words. But in fact there was considerable change. Vandals had recently destroyed a natural arch in the
river cliffs that had excited Lewis to wonder. Cattle crowding
the river banks had stripped away the thick understory of young
cottonwoods that we could still see on the small islands in the river.
There were no grizzly bears in the bottomland thickets, the wolves

had been eradicated, and the bison displaced by herds of cattle. But the river still flowed along past the islands and sandbars beneath the white cliffs, resplendent in the summer sun. This place surely needed protection and a plan for restoring the riparian forest and native wildlife.

We waded ashore in late afternoon and pulled our canoes from the water. By then Ambrose was ready to add his prestige and historical perspective to the case for a national monument. He was a Montana resident, and his endorsement could make a difference in a state where attitudes in the congressional delegation ranged from noncommittal to hostile. Right on cue he endorsed our proposal. Then as we packed up to return to Lewiston, having made our case to the press, Ambrose took his turn to make a request of me. William Clark, he explained, had never received the captain's commission that both President Jefferson and Meriwether Lewis had promised him. "President Clinton has the power to correct that oversight," said Ambrose. "He should give William Clark that commission."

After returning to Washington, I looked into the matter. It was not entirely clear whether Jefferson had actually promised the commission, or whether Lewis, in his eagerness to recruit Clark, had gone overboard in promising a commission and leading Clark to believe that he had the authority to do so. Whatever the facts, Lewis and Clark went on to raise the American flag on Pacific shores and return safely, together completing one of the most important and inspiring journeys of exploration in recorded history.

On January 17, 2001, President Clinton made his last public appearance in the East Room of the White House. The occasion was a proclamation establishing the Upper Missouri River Breaks National Monument. Then, in the presence of several of Clark's descendants, he awarded the great explorer his commission, captain in the Corps of Discovery.

This was no time to hand the outgoing president another tally card, but it would have recorded that he had issued more national monument proclamations than Theodore Roosevelt and had by some measures protected more acres of land and water than any of his predecessors.

Our public lands are a singular American treasure, handed down to us by generations of conservationists and public officials, including both Republicans and Democrats. From time to time this bipartisan consensus has been challenged, on occasion by a president, more often within the Congress. Today, however, our public land institutions are under unprecedented attack from both the president and the Congress. This is a season for all Americans to take renewed interest in defending their heritage—the freedom and glory of wide open public spaces.

Epilogue

~~~ ~~~ ~~~ ~~~ ~~~ ~~~ ~~~

In 1967 a series appeared in the *New Yorker* written by John McPhee about a little-known region in southeastern New Jersey called the Pine Barrens. It was a landscape apart, nearly a million acres of sand hills, pine forests, cedar bottoms, blueberry thickets, and cranberry bogs, where residents lived and worked on the land in communities dating back to colonial times. McPhee portrayed their history, recounted their legends, told their stories and folklore, weaving it all into an eloquent requiem for a way of life and landscape seemingly about to disappear.

The Pine Barrens were threatened by geography, specifically their proximity to New York City less than seventy miles to the north and Philadelphia less than fifty miles to the west. Speculators and real-estate promoters were at work subdividing the forests into thousands of unimproved lots, and plans were circulating for a supersonic jetport covering more than thirty-two thousand acres. Traveling through the region, McPhee foresaw the day when the

Pine Barrens would merge into "a great unbroken eastern city, extending from Boston to Richmond."

McPhee encountered local conservationists who were disorganized and dispirited, and he concluded that little could be done to save the region from the bulldozers: "given the great numbers and the crossed purposes of all the big and little powers that would have to work together to accomplish anything on a major scale in the pines, it would appear that the Pine Barrens are not very likely to be the subject of dramatic decrees or acts of legislation. They seem to be headed slowly to extinction."

However, that did not happen. In 1968 the New Yorker articles came out in book form as The Pine Barrens, which became a national best seller. New Jersey residents began demanding action to save what remained. McPhee had awakened the public just as in Florida, Marjory Stoneman Douglas had sounded the call to save the Everglades.

Ten years later, in 1978, at the request of the New Jersey delegation, Congress made a most unusual offer to the state: develop a comprehensive land use plan for the Pine Barrens, pass it by the secretary of the interior for approval, and the state would be entitled to draw down twenty-six million dollars in federal grants for plan preparation and land acquisition.

Governor Brendan Byrne responded by creating the Pinelands Commission, made up of one member selected by each of the seven counties within the Pinelands region, seven additional members appointed by the governor, and one by the secretary of the interior. The New Jersey legislature promptly confirmed the commission in law and empowered it to create a comprehensive land use plan designating permanent areas for agriculture, forestry, nature preserves, and development within the existing communities.

To gain support from cranberry and blueberry farmers, whose land the resulting legislation placed off-limits to future development, a system of transferable development rights was created whereby developers within urban areas can obtain zoning for increased density only by purchasing "development credits" from the owners of farmlands designated for protection. A developer can increase density by eight additional housing units by purchasing development rights from thirty-nine acres of farmland for the going rate of approximately thirty-five thousand dollars.

Today the Pinelands communities continue to grow at the same rate as the rest of New Jersey. The overall landscape patterns, however, remain largely unchanged—a mosaic of forests, farmlands, and dispersed communities. Public support for the Pinelands plan continues to be strong, and the region is regularly referenced and discussed as a model of effective regional land use planning. How might the Pinelands example be compared and contrasted to the experiences related elsewhere in this book?

The Everglades experience seems most like the Pinelands. In each case the process of change was initiated by grassroots demand, subsequently amplified by writers giving voice to a strong regional identity. In both cases effective governors championed the cause. And in both cases legislation helped to create effective federal-state partnerships. Florida began by enacting the Everglades Forever Act, which was followed by congressional passage of comprehensive Everglades restoration legislation. In New Jersey federal legislation came first, establishing the Pinelands National Reserve, and was followed by the New Jersey Pinelands Commission legislation.

Not every region will receive such special consideration. Congress is unlikely to tailor a special law for each of the many landscapes and watersheds within our vast continental nation that merit our attention. Therefore we must have at hand generic national laws, available to be used at all times and in many places. The Endangered Species Act, discussed in chapter 2, demonstrates how the application of one such law created preserves in Southern California, helped evolve an urban boundary around Las Vegas, and prompted a countywide open space plan in Tucson and Pima

County. These examples from the Southwest also clearly illustrate, in somewhat different ways, the critical importance, not just of federal leadership, but of participation from state and local governments, ideally beginning with the governor, but at the very least involving committed local officials.

Farmlands are the bridge between city and wilderness and that bridge is often not very stable. Cities sprawl, cannibalizing valuable farmland. And farmlands in turn expand outward, devouring savannas and forests and wetlands. The Pinelands Comprehensive Plan provides needed stability by drawing boundaries—around urban areas to protect agriculture and around agriculture to protect the forests and wetlands. Chapter 3 explores how these lessons might be applied on a large scale to restore a better balance between agriculture and the natural landscape.

Chapter 4, tracing the sinuous relationships between water and land, leads us to recognize that, to be truly effective, land use plans must be conceived as land-and-water use plans. The shallow Cohansey and Kirkwood aquifers underlying the Pinelands feed numerous rivers that are among the few uncontaminated waters remaining on the East Coast. The Pinelands Comprehensive Plan demonstrates how land can be managed to preserve water quality, a task that we must now undertake in the nation at large.

The fundamental issue facing public lands, discussed in chapter 5, is that we have yet to reach consensus as to their ultimate placement on the use spectrum from cities to wilderness—whether they are to be, like farmland, for resource uses such as livestock grazing and timber cutting, or are to be retained primarily for wilderness values. The argument made in this book is that public lands should now be administered primarily, although not exclusively, to maintain and restore their natural values. The Pinelands, with the exception of several military bases and one wildlife refuge, are not federal lands; and the Pinelands Comprehensive Plan does not directly inform public lands issues, with one important exception: whether in New Jersey or in Nevada, whether on public or private lands, the imperative for good land use planning is public involvement and active participation from all levels of government—federal, state, and local.

A basic measure of good land use is sustainability, a word that has come to signify living in a respectful relationship with the land, passing it on unimpaired, and even renewed and restored, to future generations. Development should enlarge the possibilities for human progress, creativity, and quality of life, which it cannot accomplish by continually eroding the beauty and productivity of the natural world. The Pinelands story is a reminder that we can promote progress even as we preserve our history, our culture, and the integrity of the natural world in which we live.

Selected Readings

Chapter 1. Everglades Forever

Douglas, Marjory Stoneman. *The Everglades: River of Grass*. New York: Rinehart, 1947. The classic account.

Grunwald, Michael. *The Swamp: The Story of the Everglades*. New York: Simon and Schuster, 2005. Includes a comprehensive discussion of contemporary restoration issues.

Leopold, Aldo. *A Sand County Almanac, and Sketches Here and There*. New York: Oxford University Press, 1949. A classic in nature writing, asserting the need for an "ecological conscience."

Wilson, E. O. *The Diversity of Life*. Cambridge, MA: Belknap Press, 1992. Along with Leopold, a basic work on ecology relevant to the issues I discuss in all chapters.

Chapter 2. Cities in the Wilderness

Fulton, William. *The Reluctant Metropolis: The Politics of Urban Growth in Los Angeles*. Point Arena, CA: Solano Press Books, 1997. A very readable, wide-ranging discussion of planning in Southern California, including a chapter on the gnatcatcher controversy.

Layzer, Judith A. *The Environmental Case: Translating Values into Policy*. Washington, D.C.: CQ Press, 2002. A classroom-oriented text with detailed descriptions of the Southern California gnatcatcher issues, as well as the Everglades and the western grazing issues.

National Research Council, Committee on the Formation of the National Biological Survey. *A Biological Survey for the Nation*. Washington, D.C.: National Academy Press, 1993. Makes the case for a national biological information program.

Petersen, Shannon. *Acting for Endangered Species: The Statutory Ark*. Lawrence: University Press of Kansas, 2002. Recounts the history of the Endangered Species Act.

Whyte, William H. *The Last Landscape*. Garden City, NY: Doubleday, 1968. An early discussion of landscape from an urban perspective.

Wolch, Jennifer, Manuel Pastor Jr., and Peter Dreier, eds. *Up Against the Sprawl: Public Policy and the Making of Southern California*. Minneapolis: University of Minnesota Press, 2004. Essays include a discussion of local referendum and initiative measures to establish urban growth limits.

Chapter 3. What's the Matter with Iowa?

Kimbrell, Andrew, ed. *The Fatal Harvest Reader: The Tragedy of Industrial Agriculture*. Washington, D.C.: Island Press, 2002. Collects contemporary and often controversial views on agriculture policy.

Manning, Richard. *Grassland: The History, Biology, Politics and Promise of the American Prairie*. New York: Penguin Books, 1997. The best comprehensive history and discussion of prairie issues.

Wilcove, David S. *The Condor's Shadow: The Loss and Recovery of Wildlife in America*. New York: Random House, 2000. Devotes a chapter to the loss of species on the midwestern prairies.

Chapter 4. At Water's Edge

Barry, John M. *Rising Tide: The Great Mississippi Flood of 1927 and How It Changed America*. New York: Simon and Schuster, 1998. An exceptionally readable account of the 1927 flood and the ascent of the Army Corps of Engineers.

Glennon, Robert. *Water Follies: Groundwater Pumping and the Fate of America's Fresh Waters*. Washington, D.C.: Island Press, 2002. Discusses and makes recommendations for state action to manage groundwater resources.

Grossman, Elizabeth. *Watershed: The Undamming of America*. New York: Counterpoint, 2002. Recounts the recent history of dam removal.

Horton, Tom. *Turning the Tide: Saving the Chesapeake Bay*. Rev. ed. Washington, D.C.: Island Press, 2003. Explains contemporary issues concerning the bay.

Warner, William. *Beautiful Swimmers: Watermen, Crabs, and the Chesapeake Bay*. With an introduction by John Barth. New York: Penguin Books, 1987. A Pulitzer Prize–winning account of the history and culture of the bay.

Chapter 5. Land of the Free

Coggins, George C., Charles F. Wilkinson, and John D. Leshy. *Federal Public Land and Resources Law*. 5th ed. New York: Foundation Press, 2002. Textbook treatment of public lands issues.

Stegner, Wallace. *Beyond the Hundredth Meridian: John Wesley Powell and the Second Opening of the West*. Repr., New York: Penguin Books, 1992. Remains the best history of public lands and the development of government science and administration. The discussion of John Wesley Powell and his irrigation survey is an instructive account of an early attempt at rational planning for the use of land and water in the arid west.

Wilkinson, Charles F. *Crossing the Next Meridian: Land, Water, and the Future of the West.* Washington, D.C.: Island Press, 1992. The best introduction to contemporary public lands issues.

Acknowledgments

The research for this book comes largely from the field, accumulated in the course of working with many dedicated and talented
employees of the Department of the Interior. While I cannot in this
limited space thank them all by name, I must acknowledge those
directly engaged in the events described in these pages.

I knew very little about the Florida Everglades when I arrived at
Interior, where I encountered some excellent teachers, including
Dick Ring, superintendent of Everglades National Park; Colonel
Rock Salt of the Army Corps of Engineers and subsequently direc-
tor of the Everglades task force; George Frampton; Bonnie Cohen;
Glynn Key; and Mary Doyle.

In California and the Pacific Northwest, where we worked out
applications of the Endangered Species Act, I had assistance from
Mike Spear, Mike Heyman, Tom Collier, John Garamendi, Don
Barry, Marc Ebbin, Jay Ziegler, and two directors of the Fish and
Wildlife Service, Jamie Clark and the late Mollie Beattie. Ron Pul-
liam, Tom Lovejoy, and the late Ted LaRoe helped to bring the

National Biological Service to a safe harbor within the U.S. Geological Survey.

In the numerous western water negotiations, Betsy Rieke, Patty Beneke, and Joe Sax played important roles. Jamie Workman blazed the path toward dam removal. John Duffy, Ed Cohen, Molly McUsic, Roy Wright, Mark Squillace, and Tom Fry participated in the informal caucus leading to the creation of national monuments and protected areas.

On public lands issues, Bob Armstrong, Mike Dombeck, Dean Bibles, Ed Hastey, Elaine Zielinski, Deborah Williams, Marilyn Heiman, and Mark Stiles provided invaluable assistance. At the National Park Service, Roger Kennedy and Bob Stanton served ably, and I especially benefited from the advice of Rob Arnberger, superintendent at Grand Canyon National Park, and Bob Barbee and Mike Finley, superintendents at Yellowstone National Park during the wolf restoration period. John Duffy, Ed Cohen, and Brook Yeager assisted on all fronts.

I began this book after a brief street encounter with Chuck Savitt, who invited me to work with Island Press, promising and then delivering the help so essential to a novice author. My editor, Jonathan Cobb, provided what I most needed, early engagement in thinking out and shaping ideas, followed by gentle, persistent advice to develop the main themes while steering me away from the political digressions that afflict most Washington writers. My copy editor, Julie Van Pelt, provided many helpful lessons in use of the English language. John Leshy, Dave Hayes, Mary Doyle, Claudia O'Brien, and David Bodney all read and critiqued parts of the manuscript; I am grateful for their help, while absolving them of any responsibility for errors that will crop up in a book that draws on memory for many events now receding in time.

I am indebted beyond measure to the four individuals to whom this book is dedicated. My deputy secretary, David Hayes, brought exceptional legal, negotiating, and personal skills to many complex problems, including the Gila River Indian water settlement, subsequently enacted into law in 2004; the CalFed and Colorado River negotiations; and the Headwaters Forest acquisition, to name a few. John Leshy, solicitor for eight years, friend and advisor for more than thirty, preeminent public-lands scholar, participated in and left his imprint on every major accomplishment of our tenure. My chief of staff, Anne Shields, brought skills acquired during a career at the Department of Justice, and, most importantly, a rare ability to manage with a light touch, providing open access, encouraging the upward flow of ideas and information, making Interior a productive and fun place to work.

To my wife Hattie, I can never fully express my love and gratitude. She too served in the Clinton administration, first as ambassador to the Organization of American States and then as deputy administrator of the Agency for International Development. By the time eight years had elapsed, our two sons had departed for college and the dog was gone, leaving us time to look back with considerable satisfaction on our life together, with pride in our two fine sons, grateful for the opportunity to have served our country in such interesting and challenging assignments.

Index